Chesterfield 1991

CRICKET GROUNDS
Then and Now

William A Powell

DIAL
PRESS

First published 1994

ISBN 0 7110 2289 5

© William Powell 1994

Published by Dial Press

an imprint of Ian Allan Ltd, Terminal House, Station Approach, Shepperton, Surrey TW17 8AS. Printed by Ian Allan Printing Ltd, Coombelands House, Coombelands Lane, Addlestone, Weybridge, Surrey KT15 1HY.

In memory of my grandmother
Hameeda Malik

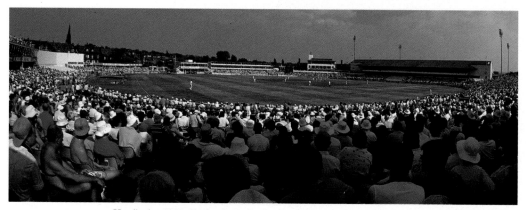

Headingley 1990, England - India Texaco Trophy match in progress.

BIBLIOGRAPHY

Homes of Sport: Cricket; N. Yardley and J. M. Kilburn, 1952.
The Watney Book of Test Match Grounds; I. Peebles, 1967.
Famous Cricket Grounds; L. W. Meynell, 1951.
Grounds of Appeal; A. Sampson, 1980.
Homes of Cricket; G. Plumtree, 1987.
Wisden Cricketers' Almanack; 1864-1993.
Association of Cricket Statisticians publications.
Wisden Cricket Monthly.
The Cricketer.
Playfair Cricket Monthly.

ABBREVIATIONS USED IN THIS BOOK

CC	Cricket Club
CCC	County Cricket Club
MCC	Marylebone Cricket Club
TCCB	Test and County Cricket Board
FC	Football Club
RFC	Rugby Football Club

ACKNOWLEDGEMENTS

The compilation of a book on a subject as diverse as first-class cricket grounds must rely on the wholehearted support and assistance of so many persons concerned with the administration of the game. I therefore acknowledge with much gratitude the co-operation over several years received from the chief executives, secretaries and administrative staff at all the cricket grounds included in this book.

I also thank Simon Forty, Peter Waller and Nick Grant of Ian Allan Publishing, Mike Willis of Aerofilms Library, Peter Powell, Ronald Harries, John Lodge and Mike Tarr for their assistance.

I acknowledge the sources of the illustrations which are many and include the county clubs, Aerofilms Limited, County Print Services, VCA, Airviews Manchester Airport, Jefferson Air Photography, Kent Messenger, Patrick Eagar, Empics, Ken Kelly and my own collection of photographs. Grateful thanks to top cricket photographer Patrick Eagar who kindly supplied the outstanding additional colour illustrations on the following pages: 1, 4, 8, 16, 20, 24, 25, 28, 45, 48, 49 and 136.

CONTENTS

LIST OF FIRST-CLASS GROUNDS

MARYLEBONE CRICKET CLUB
London (Lord's)

DERBYSHIRE
Derby, Chesterfield, Ilkeston

DURHAM
Chester-le-Street, (Riverside/Ropery Lane),
Darlington Durham University, Gateshead Fell,
Hartlepool Jesmond, Stockton-On-Tees

ESSEX
Chelmsford, Colchester, Ilford
Southend-On-Sea

GLAMORGAN
Cardiff, Abergavenny, Colwyn Bay, Neath,
Pontypridd, Swansea

GLOUCESTERSHIRE
Bristol, Cheltenham College,
Gloucester (Tuffley Park/King's School)

HAMPSHIRE
Southampton, Basingstoke, Portsmouth

KENT
Canterbury, Maidstone, Tunbridge Wells

LANCASHIRE
Manchester (Old Trafford), Blackpool, Liverpool
Lytham, Southport

LEICESTERSHIRE
Leicester

MIDDLESEX
Uxbridge, Southgate

NORTHAMPTONSHIRE
Northampton, Luton

NOTTINGHAMSHIRE
Nottingham (Trent Bridge), Worksop

SOMERSET
Taunton, Bath, Weston-Super-Mare

SURREY
London (The Foster's Oval), Guildford

SUSSEX
Hove, Arundel, Eastbourne, Horsham

WARWICKSHIRE
Birmingham (Edgbaston)

WORCESTERSHIRE
Worcester, Kidderminster

YORKSHIRE
Leeds (Bass Headingley), Bradford,
Harrogate, Middlesbrough
Scarborough, Sheffield

OXFORD UNIVERSITY
Oxford (The Parks)

CAMBRIDGE UNIVERSITY
Cambridge (Fenner's)

OTHER GROUNDS

SCOTLAND
Glasgow (Hamilton Crescent)

MINOR COUNTIES
Torquay

FOREWORD

Cricket is a game with a great tradition and history of which we are all proud. Through the years lovers of our national summer game have seen numerous changes to the Laws, many refinements to the equipment used and considerable changes in the attitudes of the players which we loosely define as the Spirit of the Game. However, nothing has been more marked than the development of the grounds where cricket at the top level is played.

William Powell's latest book charts the development of the first-class grounds since the beginning of this century and will be a welcome addition to the libraries of genuine cricket historians. Mention is made not only of the improvement of the stands from where spectators can enjoy their cricket but also of the many new facilities for indoor nets and other sports and leisure activities which have been built for their members and players. Different grounds have retained their own characteristics and one of the joys for the cricket spectator is to go to visit the huge stadia of the Test Match grounds and then to spend a day at a country ground such as Arundel. The pavilions and surrounds are as varied as the pitches on which first-class cricket is played.

Between 1967 and 1984 I was fortunate to have had the opportunity to play first-class cricket for Surrey, Gloucestershire and Sussex. In that time I played at most of the grounds described in detail in this book. I am delighted to have been invited to write this Foreword and feel well qualified to recommend William Powell's excellent book because of my association with the various grounds and especially so now as Secretary of MCC. Lord's, the Home of Cricket, has seen great developments over the years and I am mindful of the responsibility of cricket administrators and architects who have the task of reviewing constantly the plans for further development.

Roger Knight
Secretary
Marylebone Cricket Club

INTRODUCTION

In this book I have attempted to include all grounds currently used for first-class matches in the British Isles in 1994.

The grounds used regularly for first-class cricket now number nearly 70 in all and vary from Lord's to the simplest of small club grounds, and from the established stadia that can accommodate some 28,000 spectators to the others that can only accommodate 2,500 with temporary facilities.

Originally it was sufficient to close mow a strip of grass in a field and provide a set of stumps to produce a setting for a game of cricket. The first addition was to be a small (usually timber) building to act as a covered changing space - the origin of today's grand pavilion. Grounds were then frequently furnished with marquees and a variety of tents, a practice which continues to this day, to provide for and enhance the facilities.

Even the founder of our most prestigious arena, Thomas Lord, is said to have moved the turf from Dorset Square to Lodge Road and thence onto St John's Wood Road as he sought to establish a permanent site for his cricket ground in London. Others have changed little since their first establishment in the 19th century.

The development of the great pavilion which was to dominate many cricket grounds was a feature of the late Victorian period and is exemplified by Trent Bridge, Nottingham 1886, Lord's, London 1889, Old Trafford, Manchester 1894 and Kennington Oval, London 1896 (the latter two by the same architect). However, all these pavilions appear to have been preceded by the substantial Liverpool Cricket Club pavilion at Aigburth cricket ground in 1880. Similarly, by the early 1880s both Oxford University Cricket Club and Cambridge University Cricket Club had pavilions superior to many of their counterparts in the counties. The Oxford pavilion sited in the University Parks has changed very little in its external appearance since its building in 1881.

Thereafter, developments proceeded apace during the Golden Age up to the outbreak of World War 1, so that already by the turn of the century critics were suggesting that Lord's Cricket Ground was becoming more like an amphitheatre.

The period between 1920 and 1939 saw a resurgence in the development of existing cricket grounds and some new ones, although the events of World War 2 with the need of sites for anti-aircraft gun emplacements and balloon barrages in urban areas saw cricket grounds - desirable open spaces which were often closed to the public - used for practices quite different to sport.

In the immediate postwar years there was a shortage of materials and the rebuilding of housing and industries had priority over less crucial requirements; further developments to cricket grounds had to wait for the 1960s and have continued through to the present day.

This introduction cannot be concluded without thanking Roger Knight, the former Cambridge University, Gloucestershire, Sussex and Surrey player and now the Secretary of the MCC, for kindly writing the foreword to this book as well as the many people who have assisted me with this work. I have tried to record all those who have made some contribution in the acknowledgements.

William Powell
Hemel Hempstead
April 1994

Photographic Note: Almost half of the illustrations in this book are aerial photographs from the archives of Aerofilms. Readers wishing to obtain copies of these may order them directly from the company quoting the negative number given alongside each photograph. Aerofilms have generously offered a 25% discount from their standard rates on orders of pictures from this book. Write to: Aerofilms Ltd, Gate Studios, Borehamwood, Herts WD6 1EJ. Copies of cricket card photographs credited to County Print Services are obtainable from 74 Walden Way, Hainault, Essex IG6 3BU

Lord's

View from the new Compton and Edrich Stands during the 1992 Natwest final between Leicestershire and Northhamptonshire.

Inset above:
This picture shows the famous club colours of the MCC with an inset of Benjamin Aislabie, the Hon Secretary of the club, between 1822 and 1842.
County Print Services

Above right:
The MCC was founded in 1787 and its early history relates directly to the development of Lord's itself. Thomas Lord, a Yorkshireman born in Thirsk in 1755, had by 1780 found his way to London where he took employment at the recreation ground at White Conduit Fields, Islington. Here he met members of the White Conduit Cricket Club, founded in 1782, who were not satisfied with the ground in Islington and suggested to Lord that he should find them a more exclusive location. This he found at Dorset Fields (Dorset Square now forms part of this area) and leased the ground from the Portman Estates.

In 1787 the first match was played here between Middlesex and Essex and the MCC was founded by Thomas Lord's patrons from the White Conduit Club headed by Lord Winchelsea.

The first match on the St John's Wood ground was played between the MCC and Hertfordshire in June 1814 and it was here that the MCC found its permanent home. In 1825 Thomas Lord had visions of developing much of the ground area for housing as the district of St John's Wood was being developed at this time. This was prevented by William Ward, a member of the club, who bought out Lord. Later, in 1835 William Ward handed over to James Dark, under whose control the ground remained until 1864 when he sold the lease to the MCC. Until recently the former sweet shop, now the souvenir clothing outlet below the New Mound Stand, retained the

name Dark's Shop. In 1860 the club had missed the opportunity to purchase the freehold but six years later it finally paid Mr Moses £18,000 for the freehold of the ground as it then existed. This precipitated the improvement and extension of the pavilion shown in this picture and a new grandstand for the public. The first full-time groundsman was also employed. It was about this time that the then Secretary, Mr R. A. Fitzgerald, introduced the now familiar red and yellow colours of the club in place of the original blue and white.
Author's collection

Far right:
In 1877 the club came to an agreement with Middlesex County Cricket Club to provide a home for the county club and this arrangement has continued ever since. While the Australians were to meet the MCC in a one-day match on

LORDS CRICKET GROUND PAVILION, LONDON, N.W.8.

HOBBS, J. B.

16·C.   SURREY

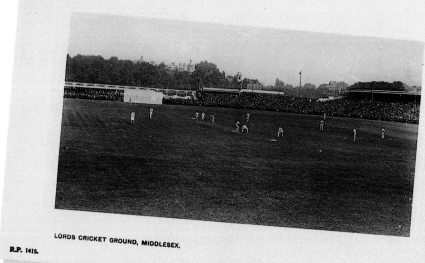

LORDS CRICKET GROUND, MIDDLESEX.

R.P. 1415.

their first tour of England in 1878, it was not until 1884 that England met Australia in a Test Match at Lord's, the Kennington Oval having led the way in staging Test cricket in the capital. This picture shows a view of Lord's during the 1905 Test Match between England and Australia with the Mound Stand and Nursery End in the background.
Author's collection

Above left:
The highest individual innings against Middlesex at Lord's is 316 no by J.B. Hobbs for Surrey in 1926.
Author's collection

9

GRACE'S GATE, LORD'S, ST. JOHN'S WOOD ROAD, LONDON

Above:

In 1923 the Grace Gates shown in this picture were erected at the entrance on St John's Wood Road and in 1934 the garden - now the traditional place for team photographs - was developed in memory of Lord Harris. The 'Q' Stand was also built at the same time and all were the work of Sir Herbert Baker. The stands at the Nursery End were also erected and the car park developed beyond the nursery ground, care being taken to retain the tree screen dividing the main ground from the nursery. 1937 saw the celebration of the club's 150th anniversary. World War 2 gave the 66-year-old Sir Pelham Warner the opportunity to take charge at Lord's as acting Secretary while Col R. S. Rait-Kerr was on war service. While the nursery ground became a barrage balloon site and Father Time was pulled down by a balloon cable, Lord's stayed open and 13,000 spectators watched a match on 10 August 1940. Lord's escaped serious damage and in 1945 international cricket recommenced, with matches against the Australians, in the 'Victory' Test, and later against the Dominions.
Author's collection

Right:
This picture shows an aerial view of Lords taken in 1922 from the Pavilion End. *Aerofilms*

10

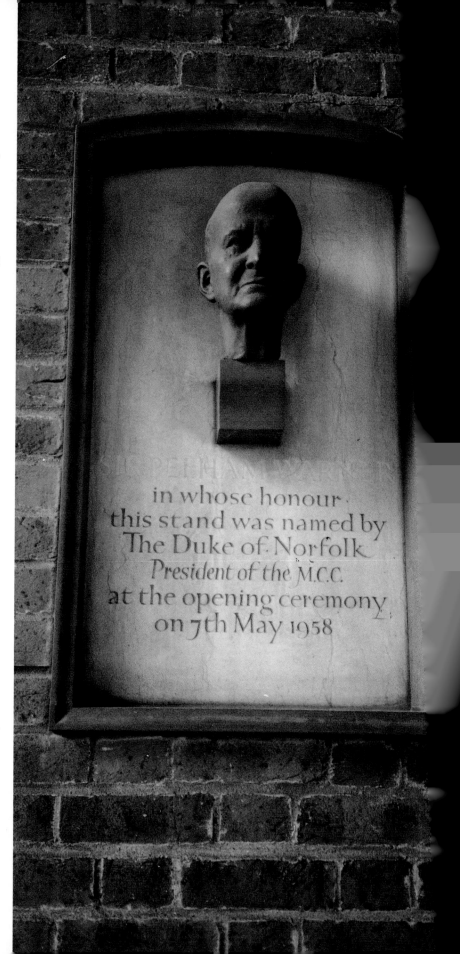

Right:

In 1945 the MCC appointed its first curator and this led to the establishment of the Memorial Gallery which was opened in 1953. Further development took place in 1958 with the building of the Warner Stand with its two levels, snack bars and press box. This was the site of the single storey 'A' enclosure between the pavilion and the grandstand. This picture shows the statue of Sir Pelham Warner, situated on the first floor stair landing near the entrance to the Warner Stand bar. In 1968 the Tavern and the adjoining buildings were demolished and replaced by the New Tavern Stand. The Tavern was re-sited adjoining the Grace Gates and the new Banqueting Suite.

By 1969 there had been big changes to the responsibilities of the MCC. Its direct control of first-class professional cricket in the United Kingdom had been handed over to the TCCB; in 1968 the National Cricket Association took over the responsibilities for amateur cricket. This left the MCC responsible only for the Laws of Cricket. The Cricket Council composed of representatives of all cricketing authorities in the United Kingdom was also established in 1968. The National Club Cricket Championship final has been staged at Lord's since 1969 and the National Village Championship final since 1972. *Author*

Above Opposite:

In 1887 the centenary of the MCC was celebrated with a dinner in the Long Room at a time when the membership, then just over 5,000, was constantly increasing. Although the grandstand had two stories of covered seating, it was realized that it would have to be replaced. A new one was built in 1889-90 designed by architect Thomas Verity (who had worked on details of the Royal Albert Hall). It stands to this day with little alteration to its external appearance, the only extensions being the professionals' changing rooms and the press box adjoining the north end which have since been converted to a members' bar and the MCC offices. This picture shows the pavilion and the 'Q' Stand with a match in progress. Shortly afterwards the club purchased a

in whose honour this stand was named by The Duke of Norfolk President of the M.C.C. at the opening ceremony on 7th May 1958

S.20168.

LORDS

nursery garden at the eastern end of the ground, but no sooner had this been done than the Manchester and Sheffield Railway Company attempted to buy the area for the development of the railway line from Marylebone Station. After due consideration the club relinquished the freehold of the strip of land bordering Wellington Road - currently the members' car park area - and received in exchange the site of the Clergy Orphan School to the south, where the MCC Indoor Cricket School and main MCC Souvenir Shop are now located. *Author's collection*

Right:
The Lord's Tavern is now situated next to the Grace Gates adjoining the Banqueting Suite, while this picture shows a view of the Tavern as it was in 1948. At the Nursery End in addition to the members' car park and nursery practice area where players take nets and the Cross Arrows Cricket Club plays during September there is the MCC Indoor Cricket School and School Cricket Shop where cricket coaching and equipment can be obtained throughout the year.
Author's collection

Following page:
Both Thomas Lord and his ground prospered as Lord's became the principal cricket venue in London, which then had a population of little more than 750,000. The MCC inherited from Hambledon Cricket Club the responsibility for governing the game throughout the country and 200 years later it still retains power to make the Laws of Cricket. It was not too long, however, before the expansion of the built-up area of London forced Lord and the MCC to move in 1810 to another ground in the area south of the present Lodge Road. This did not prove a popular ground and in 1812 the decision to construct the Regents Canal forced Lord to make a second move. He took with him on each occasion, it is said, the turf from the original pitch. This picture shows an aerial view of Lord's in 1927; the land between the Regents Canal and the ground - where the power station stands - was where Lord's second ground was sited. *Aerofilms*

View of the ground and pavilion during a match on the West Indies' tour in 1991.

Top right:

While so many of the MCC's public duties have been transferred to other bodies, it remains a large private club with some 18,000 members (and a substantial waiting list). Its ground is still to most cricket lovers worldwide the spiritual home of the great game. In 1987 the club celebrated its bicentenary and marked this by the complete redevelopment of the Mound Stand and the erection of the Bicentenary Gates on the St John's Wood Road side of the ground. This picture shows the stone which recorded this opening in May 1987. During 1989-91 the stands at the Nursery End have been reconstructed following their naming in 1989 as the Compton and Edrich Stands. The new stands were opened on 27 May 1991 by Denis Compton and Justin Edrich (son of Bill Edrich) during the luncheon interval of the third Texaco Trophy one-day international between England and the West Indies. The well-publicised delays to this construction did not prevent the reconstruction winning the Concrete Society's 1991 building category award. The architects were Michael Hopkins & Partners who were also responsible for the New Mound Stand. The ground is now truly closer to the amphitheatre

which had first been a criticism in 1903. This picture shows a view of the Compton and Edrich Stands from the pavilion during the Middlesex and Sussex Axa Equity & Law Sunday League match in 1993.

In 1989 the 'Q' Stand was renamed the Sir George Allen Stand and now includes at the lower level an enclosed Middlesex CCC members' room, from which cricket can be viewed and refreshments taken. This picture shows a view of the pavilion and 'Q' Stand in 1993. Author

All the buildings at the ground are permanent. The pavilion is the centrepiece and includes the famous Long Room shown in this 1991 picture. The members and their guests also have exclusive use of the Warner Stand, the upper and lower Tavern Stand and the Sir George Allen Stand although the upper part is only available to MCC members. At the rear of the pavilion is the MCC Memorial Gallery and museum together with the library, squash and real tennis courts. At the back of this building is the TCCB headquarters and NCA offices. To the south is the Lord Harris Memorial Garden and the Middlesex CCC office and shop. To the rear of the Warner

Stand is the Coronation Garden, where members can picnic during luncheon intervals. *Author*

Far right:

Expansion continued apace in the 20th century and the club was to acquire new responsibilities. In 1898 the Board of Control was set up under the chairmanship of the President of the MCC to organize Test cricket in England. In 1904 the Advisory County Cricket Committee was founded and in 1909 England, Australia and South Africa founded the Imperial Cricket Conference. In 1903 the MCC also took over from various sponsors the responsibility of arranging and financing official England tours overseas. All these bodies had their headquarters at Lord's and still do to this day, although re-formed and completely separated administratively from the MCC in the form of the Test and County Cricket Board and the International Cricket Conference. The new grandstand was built on the north side of the ground to the designs of architect Sir Herbert Baker, who had been responsible for many public buildings including the Bank of England and India House. He also presented the

Father Time' weather vane to the MCC: it has become an internationally known landmark. This picture shows a view of the pavilion, old 'A' enclosure and the grandstand with a match in progress. *Author's collection*

Above:
The highest individual innings for Middlesex at Lord's is 277 no by E.H. Hendren versus Kent in 1922.
Author's collection

HENDREN, E. H.

176-C   MIDDLESEX

S.20167.

LORDS CRICKET GROUND, LONDON, N.W.8.

17

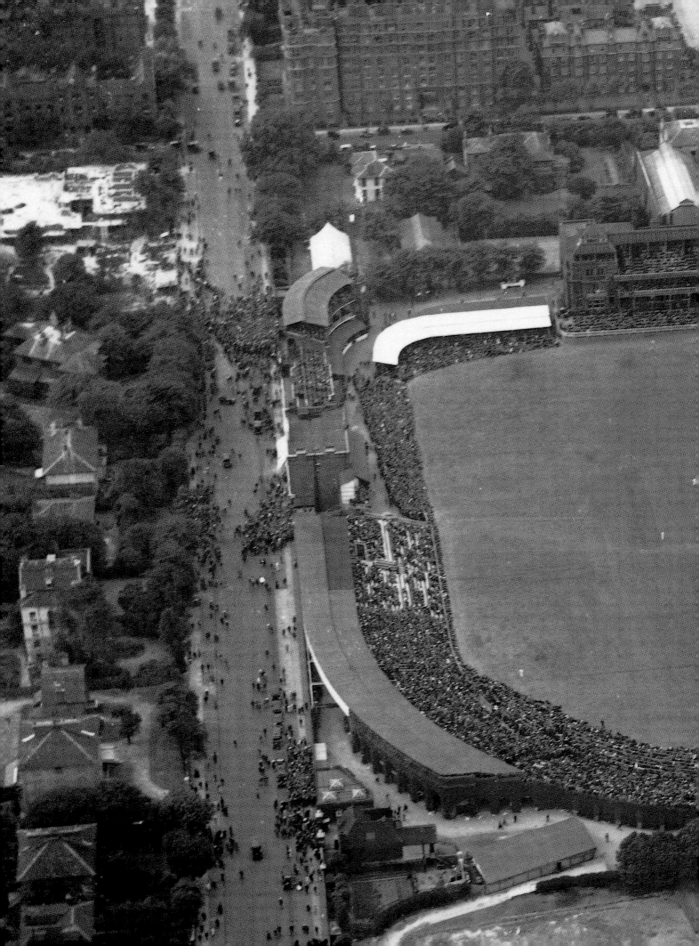

The new Compton and Edrich Stands, with play in progress during the second Test against the West Indies in 1991.

Previous page:
This picture shows an aerial view taken in 1922 from the Nursery End. *Aerofilms*

Above and Right:
It is said that certain of the excavations from the tunnels below the Wellington Road side of the ground provided banking for the original Mound Stand built in 1898-99 on the area which was previously the old tennis and racket courts; these were rebuilt at the rear of the pavilion. Already critics were likening the ground to an amphitheatre and suggesting that Thomas Lord would 'turn in his grave' at its transformation. these pictures illustrate the Mound Stand as it was in 1920 and the splendid New Mound Stand taken in 1991.

Above:
The highest individual innings at Lord's in a first-class match is 333 by Graham Gooch, recorded for England versus India during the second Test Match of 1990. *County Print Services*

Left:
The current ground capacity after improvements in 1989-91 is now set at 28,000 and this has been achieved for all the popular matches staged since including the Texaco Trophy, Test Matches, Benson and Hedges Cup and National Westminster Bank Trophy finals. The stands are numbered A to Q from the Warner Stand in a clockwise direction around to the Sir George Allen Stand. This picture shows an aerial view of the ground in 1989 during the construction stage of the Compton and Edrich Stands at the Nursery End of the ground. *Aerofilms*

23

G. O. Allan. 64

Above:
The best bowling performance in an innings for Middlesex at Lord's is 10 for 40 by G. O. B. Allen versus Lancashire in 1929. *Author*

Top:
A view of the ground during the England versus the West Indies Texaco Trophy match in 1991.

Left:
The new Mound Stand taken in 1991 during the second test against the West Indies.

Derbyshire

DERBYSHIRE

A view of the ground at Chesterfield during the Gillette Cup match between Derby and Middlesex in 1991

Above:

The grandstand, complete with a copper-domed viewing cupola, stables and jockeys' quarters, was used for players dressing rooms until the modern Lund Pavilion was built. This picture shows a view of the ground in 1992.

The present ground occupies an area of 17 acres and in 1982 a 125 year lease was purchased from the owners, Derby City Council, thanks to a generous loan from the local authority and the proceeds from winning the National Westminster Bank Trophy in 1981. Since that year much building has taken place including the Lund Pavilion and sponsors' lounges.

The extent of the redevelopment has been the Lund Pavilion including a new enlarged scoreboard, the Butterley and the Steetley Stands, the Derbyshire Supporters' Club Room, Tea Room and Derbyshire CCC Souvenir Shop. In 1991 there were plans to construct a hotel, sports centre and light industrial development but lack of finances and a downturn in the property market stopped this. The largest crowd to attend a first-class match at Derby was 14,500 in 1948 for the match against the touring Australians. *Author*

Top:
The club badge of Derbyshire CCC.
County Print Services

Above:
First used in 1863 by the South Derbyshire Club and by Derbyshire CCC in 1871, the ground occupied part of the former Derby racecourse. The pitch used to be located in the centre of the racecourse but in 1939, when racing ceased due to poor crowds and finances, the wicket and playing area moved to its present position. Initially it was known as the Racecourse Ground until officials became anxious that it should be renamed the County Cricket Ground. This picture shows an aerial view in 1947. *Aerofilms*

Right:
The grandstand was built in 1911, as shown on a stone tablet below the main entrance. *Author*

Below:

The famous twisted spire of All Saints' Church, 238ft high, looks down upon Queen's Park where so much cricket history has been made. The ground was laid out in 1897 to celebrate Queen Victoria's Diamond Jubilee and Queen's Park has remained a recreational ground for the people of Chesterfield ever since.

The ground was first used by Derbyshire CCC in 1898 when Yorkshire visited. Derbyshire's most scenic ground is sited on a marked slope towards the Boating Lake End and is very pleasantly situated within the trees and shrubs of the beautiful parkland. This picture shows a view of the ground taken from the pavilion enclosure in 1988.

The home of Chesterfield Cricket Club, Queen's Park is owned and maintained by the Borough Council. The ground is circular and was at one time surrounded by a banked cycle track. The pavilion, is half-timbered and was constructed in 1897 and it, the green painted score box and the press box are the only permanent buildings on the ground. The best attendance at Chesterfield was 14,000 for the County Championship match with Yorkshire in 1948.

This picture shows an aerial view of the ground in 1963. *Aerofilms*

Right:
The highest individual innings against Derbyshire in a first-class match at Derby is 273 no by E. G. Hayes for Surrey in 1904. *Author's collection*

Below right:
The highest individual innings for Derbyshire in a first-class match at Chesterfield is 229 and was recorded by the first West Indian to play county cricket, C. A. Ollivierre, versus Essex in 1904. *Author's collection*

COUNTY CRICKETERS.

E. G. HAYES,
SURREY.

COUNTY CRICKETERS.

MR. C. A. OLLIVIERRE,
DERBYSHIRE.

The ground at Derby during the 1993
Benson & Hedges Cup match against
Northamptonshire.

Far right
The highest innings total recorded against
Derbyshire in a first-class match at Ilkeston
was 443 by the touring South Africans in
1935. *Author's collection*

Right:
The highest individual innings for
Derbyshire in a first-class match at Derby is
238 no by T. S. Worthington versus Sussex
in 1937. *Author's collection*

DERBY

PLAYER'S CIGARETTES

T. S. WORTHINGTON

THE SOUTH AFRICAN CRICKET TEAM.

Reading Left to Right : S. J. Snooke, B. Mitchell, A. B. C. Langton, C. L. Vincent, D. Tomlinson, A. D. Nourse, H. F. Wade, K. G. Viljoen, A. J. Bell, R. J. Crisp, E. L. Dalton, X. L. Balaskas, H. B. Cameron, E. A. Rowan.

ILKESTON

Previous page:

The home of Ilkeston Rutland Cricket Club was established in 1829 when - thanks to the Duke of Rutland - the club moved from Market Street to the saucer-shaped ground in the Pimlico district of the town. Eight years later it was leased to Ilkeston Corporation on the understanding that it would be developed for recreational purposes. When King George V visited Ilkeston in 1914 the ground was given to the corporation to commemorate his visit. This picture shows an aerial view in 1928. *Aerofilms*

Right:

The highest individual innings for Derbyshire in a first-class match at Ilkeston is 217 by the formidable South African all-rounder Eddie Barlow versus Surrey in 1978. *County Print Services*

Below:

Derbyshire CCC played its initial first-class match against neighbours Nottinghamshire at Ilkeston in 1925. The ground is now owned by Erewash District Council which maintains the whole area. The ground extends to 20 acres and the only permanent buildings on the ground are the pavilion shown in this picture, built after World War 1, and the scoreboard/groundsman's store. The largest crowd at Ilkeston was 10,000 for the County Championship match against Nottinghamshire in 1948. This picture shows an aerial view in 1972. *Aerofilms*

E. J. Barlow
South Africa

Durham

DURHAM

Above:
The first important match to be staged at Chester-le-Street by Durham CCC was against the touring New Zealanders in June 1927. The Chester-le-Street Cricket Club was established in 1834 and the club moved to its present ground in the late 1890s. Its original ground was near the River Wear, close to where Durham CCC's new headquarters ground is being constructed at the new Riverside County Ground complex.

Spectators have a splendid view of the playing area from the pavilion and Lumley Castle on the hillside opposite. The ground falls slightly away from the pavilion towards the castle side.

The largest crowd was 5,000 for the Gillette Cup match with Surrey in 1972. This aerial picture of Ropery Lane was taken in 1950. *Aerofilms*

Right:
The first Durham CCC Minor County Championship match to be staged at Ropery Lane, Chester-le-Street, was in August 1903 against Northumberland. This picture shows the pavilion in 1905. *Author's collection*

Top:
The club badge of Durham CCC. *County Print Services*

Above:
The Darlington Cricket Club was established in 1827 and it rented an area of ten acres to the south of the town centre at Feethams, the house where Mr J. Pease lived. Late in 1866 a new cricket ground was levelled, with the turf being transferred from the previous Park Street ground. The first Durham CCC Minor County Championship match staged at Feethams was in June 1895 against Cheshire. This picture shows a view of the ground in 1921. *Ron Harries*

Right:
The new brick cricket pavilion was constructed in 1903 by Mr T. Boyd, Darlington's principal building contractor, at an estimated cost of £900, on the site of the previous structure. The architect was Mr Fred W. Brookes. The ground was shared with Darlington Football Club which was founded in 1883 and turned professional in 1908.

The cricket and football grounds are now separated by the football stand at the Feethams End although the grounds are situated within the same complex and have the same entrance.

Darlington Borough Council contributed £20,000 in 1991 towards improving the facilities at Feethams to enable the ground to stage first-class cricket until 1995. The largest crowd was 5,000 for the matches against the South Africans in 1901 and the West Indians in 1923.

This picture shows an aerial view of the ground in 1964. *Aerofilms*

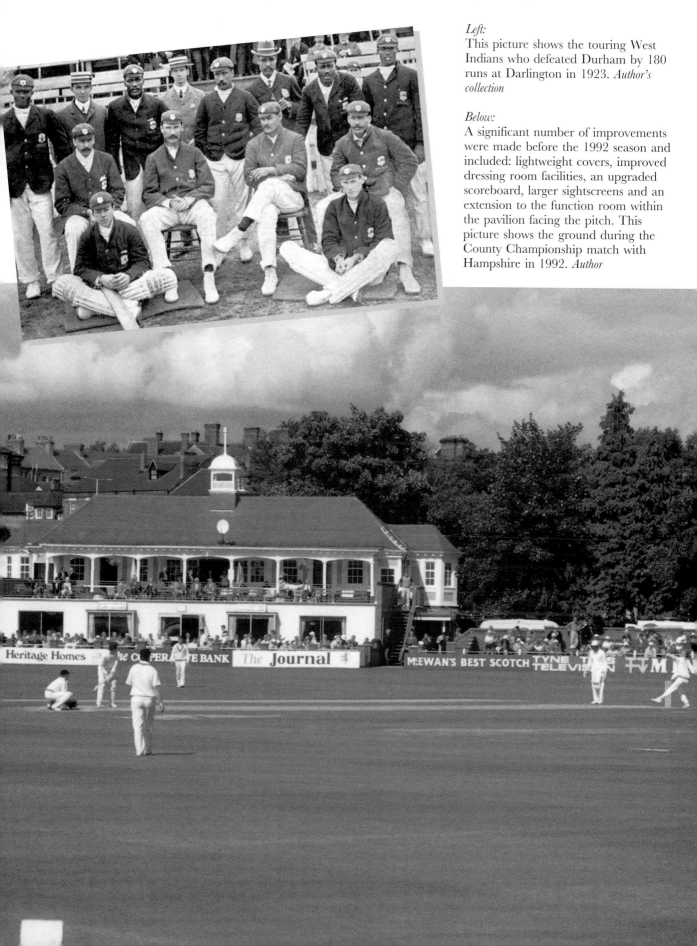

Left:
This picture shows the touring West Indians who defeated Durham by 180 runs at Darlington in 1923. *Author's collection*

Below:
A significant number of improvements were made before the 1992 season and included: lightweight covers, improved dressing room facilities, an upgraded scoreboard, larger sightscreens and an extension to the function room within the pavilion facing the pitch. This picture shows the ground during the County Championship match with Hampshire in 1992. *Author*

Above
Previously named the West Hartlepool Cricket Club, the attractive Hartlepool ground is set in parklands situated to the west side of the town. The club has been at its present headquarters since 1912 and the first Durham CCC Minor County Championship match was staged at Park Drive in June 1913 versus Lincolnshire. This picture shows the pavilion in 1992.

The general facilities at Park Drive are what you would expect at a small club ground but are being improved all the time. The ground record attendance was 4,500 for a County Championship match in 1992 against Essex. *Author*

Above right:
Established in 1816 the Stockton Cricket Club had several grounds until in 1891 its members found out that the current ground was to be turned into a park, known today as Ropner Park. The committee then found the present day ground in open fields and bought it for £1,537 2s 8d which included some levelling and drainage. In June 1892

the first match was staged there and the hosts were victorious over a team from Constable Burton near Bedale. The first Durham CCC Minor County Championship match was staged at Grangefield Road in July 1947 and in August 1952 a tablet was unveiled in the players' pavilion by the Revd R.T. Heselton MA to commemorate the names of the four members who lost their lives in World War 2. This picture shows a view of the ground and some of the permanent buildings in 1991.

The pavilion was built during the winter of 1894-95. Its basement area was used as a stable for the horses

which cut the grass and rolled the pitch until it was refurbished in 1950. The Tea Room and Croquet Pavilion were built at the turn of the century with extensions in 1950 to include a kitchen and toilets at a cost of £1,045 16s 11d; together with the scoreboard, groundsman's house and store built in 1952 for £1,560, they are the only permanent structures on the ground. The club room was named the Chris Old Room in 1980, after the Yorkshire, Warwickshire and England bowler. *Author*

Above:
This view of Durham pavilion was taken
during the game against Norfolk in 1991
– the only Minor County Championship
match staged on the ground that year.
Author

Right:
The highest individual innings for
Durham in a first-class match at Chester-
le-Street is 134 no by Victorian-born
Australian Dean Jones versus the touring
Pakistan team in 1992. Dean Jones also
recorded a second century of 105 during
the match. *VCA*

Below:
The Racecourse Ground is situated between Green Lane and the River Wear in a large bowl with splendid views of the city of Durham, the castle and the cathedral towards the west and the Durham countryside to the north and east. This aerial picture shows the ground in 1948 during the Durham Miners Gala staged at the venue where Durham CCC played its first home County Championship match against Leicestershire in 1992. *Aerofilms*

The ground capacity of 12,000 was achieved during the Durham versus Australia Tetley Bitter Tour match in 1993.

Left:
This picture shows Ian Botham who played his last first-class match at the Racecourse Ground for Durham against the touring Australians in 1993 *Author*

Above:
The Gateshead Fell Cricket Club was established in 1878 and the ground sited in Eastwood Gardens first staged a Durham CCC Minor County Championship match in June 1959 against Staffordshire. This picture shows a view of the ground in 1974. *Aerofilms*

Inset:
Gateshead Fell CC moved to their present ground during 1880/81. The ground saw regular improvements - particularly after a fire in 1966 which destroyed the pavilion and dressing rooms. These were replaced during the winter ready for the 1967 season. Eastwood Gardens in 1991. The members' clubhouse bar and lounge, the building to the east of the pavilion

with the club badge and the year 1878 depicted in blue above the entrance, was extended in 1976. The largest attendance was 5,500 for the County Championship match with Lancashire in 1992. *Author*

Below:

The Northumberland County Cricket Ground was opened in 1887 and was initially known as the new Recreation Ground for the Newcastle Police Constabulary. It is situated behind All Saints' Cemetery and approached from Lovers' Lane. The ground was acquired by the county club in March 1897 and its first Minor County Championship match was in June 1897 versus Durham. This picture shows a view of Jesmond in 1980 during the Minor Counties Cricket Association match with the West Indian tourists.
Northumberland CCC

Right

Improvements took place in 1897 and 1898 including the building of terrace seating areas at the Osborne Road End next to the Swiss chalet pavilion. This had been built for the Queen Victoria Jubilee Exhibition on the town moor in 1887 and was transferred to the ground to serve as a members' pavilion after the exhibition ended. This picture shows the pavilion during the exhibition prior to its move to Jesmond.
Northumberland CCC

The Swiss chalet pavilion was demolished in March 1962 and a new one constructed at a cost of £25,000. It was ready for the start of the 1963 season and was opened in June 1963 by Mr R.H. Houston during the Bank Holiday Minor County Championship match with Durham. This picture shows a view of the pavilion in 1992. The Callers-Pegasus Cricket Festival has been held at Jesmond since 1981 and includes two matches in early August each season. The ground capacity is 3,500 which is achieved for the majority of festival and limited-overs matches.

Essex

ESSEX

Below right:
New Writtle Street has been the headquarters of Essex CCC since the move from Leyton in 1967 with the majority of the home matches being staged there except for festival matches at Ilford, Colchester and Southend-on-Sea. The ground had been used previously by Essex from 1926 to 1939, from 1946 to 1948 and between 1950 and 1956 when it was rented annually from the Wenley Trust. The first first-class match to be staged at New Writtle Street was in 1925 versus Oxford University with the first County Championship match versus Somerset in 1926. This aerial picture shows a view of the ground in 1938. *Aerofilms*

Above right:
The ground is situated barely half a mile from where the Rivers Chelmer and Can meet and the latter passes alongside the ground at the rear of the Tom Pearce Stand. The club was assisted by a loan from the Warwickshire County Cricket Supporters' Club which enabled Essex to purchase New Writtle Street for £15,000.

Significant development has taken place since the 1960s including the construction of a pavilion, completed in 1970, and other stands. All the facilities are now permanent. The ground was without a permanent scoreboard until 1981 when an attractive building, including a groundsman's store, was built by Wimpey Construction. This picture shows a view of the pavilion in 1991 with play in progress during the Essex versus West Indies Tetley Bitter tour match.

1990 saw the construction of the Memorial Gates at the New Writtle Street main entrance to the ground and the partial covering of the popular seats on the hospital side for the general public enclosure.

Crowds of 6,500-7,500 are usual and the present ground capacity is 9,500.

A compact ground by the standards of the usual spaciousness of county ground headquarters, much has been made of the limited space available. The ground slopes slightly from south-east to north-west and since the installation of a drainage system in 1982 is known as one of the best-drained grounds on the county circuit. Previously the ground was liable to flooding because of the proximity of the River Can and the high water table. The cricket field was for some time used as an emergency helicopter pad for the nearby hospital, until the casualty department was moved elsewhere in the town. This picture shows a view of the ground taken from the Hayes Close End in 1993. *Author*

Top:
The club badge of Essex CCC. *County Print Services*

Below:

The home of the Colchester and East Essex Cricket Club, Castle Park is located off Catchpool Road very close to the River Colne, which flows around the ground at the southern end. Essex CCC first staged a County Championship match at Castle Park in 1914 against Worcestershire. The ground had to wait 20 years for its next County Championship match but after World War 2 it saw regular use for an annual festival, usually in August. Castle Park is the second ground to be used by Essex CCC in Colchester. The Military Garrison A ground was used between 1920 and 1931, in 1958 due to flooding at Castle Park, in 1966 and

from 1969 to 1972. Castle Park is susceptible to flooding because of the high water table. The ground is sited near the Castle Mound from which parkland slopes away to the rich meadows of the valley and the cricket field. Castle Park also seems to suffer from unusually poor weather, well recorded in the Colchester club's

history. In 1958 on the third day of the County Championship match with Leicestershire the playing area and surrounds were totally submerged in water; chairs and boundary boards floated across the field and the club secretary had to use waders to get about! The pavilion was constructed in 1909 ready for the 1910 season.

This picture shows the pavilion in its first year of use. Note the close proximity to the nearby River Colne. *Author*

Bottom:

This 1988 picture shows how little things have changed since 1910. The best crowd for a first-class match at Castle Park was 8,000 for the County Championship match with Middlesex in 1947. *Author*

Left:

The highest individual innings against Essex in a first-class match and the only occurrence of a player recording two double centuries in the same first-class match was achieved by Arthur Fagg of Kent at Colchester in 1938 when he scored 244 and 202 no. *Author's collection*

Cricket Pavilion, Castle Park

COLCHESTER

Above:
Ilford cricket ground sits within the 136-acre Valentine's Park which used to surround the home of a Mrs Ingleby. It was from her that the Ilford Cricket Club obtained a lease in 1897 on approximately eight acres to make the present ground. Her only condition was that the pavilion should be built under the trees. A few years later she also insisted that the sightscreens be lowered so that they could not be seen from the windows of her home. In 1899 Ilford Council purchased a large part of the parkland and lake and in 1906, when Mrs Ingleby died, they bought the rest, including her house. Ilford CC was founded in 1879 and the ground is also regularly used by Ilford and Woodford RAFA, formerly RAFA (Ilford), which was established in 1951. Essex CCC first played a first-class match at Ilford in 1923 against the West Indies tourist team. The cricket ground lies to the

west side of Valentine's Park and today is the property of the Redbridge Borough Council which maintains the ground. The annual Ilford cricket week is eagerly awaited by the local cricket fraternity for the ground ranks as one of the most picturesque in the country.

The terracing along the Cranbrook Road side of the ground was built in 1949 ready for the visit of Glamorgan, the 1948 County Champions. A crowd of 13,000, including members, was present on the Saturday of this match which is still the ground's largest attendance to watch a day's play. Since World War 2 the groundsman has kept the middle of the square entirely free from use until the festival week.

This picture shows an aerial view in 1973. *Aerofilms*

Inset:
The pavilion and secondary scoreboard in 1994. *Author*

Below:
The highest individual innings for Essex in a first-class match at Ilford is 215 by the present captain of Pakistan, Salim Malik, versus Leicestershire in 1991. *County Print Services*

Below:

Essex CCC made its first visit to Southchurch Park in 1906 for a match against Leicestershire. Essex has played at Southchurch Park each season since 1914 except for 1959, 1962, 1965 and 1967. Since 1977 all matches staged by the county in the seaside resort have been played at Southchurch Park; before then Chalkwell Park at nearby Westcliff-On-Sea had sometimes been used to stage home matches. Southchurch Park was favoured because it accommodates greater crowds and has plenty of space surrounding the playing area. However in 1989 the wicket was reported to the TCCB as being unfit for first-class cricket by the umpires during the County Championship match against Yorkshire. This cost the home side 24 points and dashed its hopes of winning the Championship. The picture shows an aerial view of the ground in 1955.
Aerofilms

Below right:

There are two pavilions at Southchurch Park - one is for the players and officials and the other belongs to the Southend Hockey Club which plays on the ground during the winter months. It is also the home ground of the Southend Cricket Club, established in 1874. Southend has played here since 1895 and the cricket pavilion was built in 1929. Southchurch Park is now owned and maintained by Southend Borough Council. Incidentally, it was in the ownership of the monks of Christ Church Canterbury from AD 823 and it was on the Southchurch foreshore that the cultivation of oysters is said to have started. The ground is sufficiently large to allow two club games to be played simultaneously. There are three separate cricket squares, of which the central one is used exclusively by the

county for matches during the Southend Festival week which usually takes place in July. The ground is a quiet park barely half a mile from the seafront, the crowded beach and a large boating lake. The largest crowd to attend a day's play at Southchurch Park was 16,000 for the visit of the 1948 Australians. The crowd saw a fine day with the visitors amassing 721 including Don Bradman's 187 scored in 125 minutes. This 1988 view from the Northumberland Avenue End shows the two pavilions with play in progress.
Author

Glamorgan

GLAMORGAN

St Helen's Swansea, during a Benson & Hedges
Cup match in 1979

Above right:
The club badge of Glamorgan CCC.
County Print Services

Above:

The home of Abergavenny Cricket Club (established in 1834), the ground is located in Avenue Road and is known to locals as Pen-y-Pound. One of the most attractive grounds on the county circuit, it is set in idyllic surroundings at the foot of the Sugar Loaf Mountain, within the Brecon Beacons National Park. Glamorgan CCC made its initial first-class county championship visit in 1983 when Worcestershire provided the opposition. The 4.5-acre Avenue Road ground was opened in 1896 with a match between a South Wales XI and an Abergavenny XI. The pavilion was rebuilt in 1977 following a fire and now has ample amenities. The clock over the entrance door survived the fire; its plaque states that it was presented to the club by Mr and Mrs Lyons in 1921.

Abergavenny CC moved from one ground to another during its early years until in 1895 an approach was made to the Marquess of Abergavenny, a keen follower of cricket and a one-time-President of Kent CCC, who leased the Avenue Road to the club. The ground took its name from the nearby Pen-y-Pound lane. The marquess provided the original pavilion in 1915 after generously giving further land in 1910 and again in 1912. This aerial picture shows a view of the ground in 1929. The new electronic scoreboard was built in memory of Mr Bill McPherson who had been groundsman for many years. Crowds at Abergavenny have been good when the weather has been kind and in 1988 some 5,000 attended the Worcestershire County Championship match. *Aerofilms*

A. R. BUTCHER

Above right:
The highest individual innings for Glamorgan in a first-class match at Abergavenny is 135 by Alan Butcher versus Leicestershire in 1987.
County Print Services

Below:

Founded in 1924, the Colwyn Bay Cricket Club has played all its home matches at Penrhyn Avenue. Glamorgan played its first first-class match at Colwyn Bay in 1966 against Derbyshire. Other notable games before this date include Wales's games against the South African tourists in 1929 and the Minor Counties Cricket Association in 1930. The Penrhyn Avenue ground has been used by teams other than Wales for Minor County Championship matches, including during the period from 1930 to 1935 by Denbighshire. The pavilion is situated to the south-east of the playing area and was built by voluntary subscriptions in recognition of those members who gave service to their country in World War 2. It was opened by HRH The Duke of Gloucester in June 1960. Wilfred Wooller was brought up in Rhos-on-Sea and it is thanks to his influence that

county cricket came to North Wales. Mr Wooller's grandfather had built the original pavilion which was opened by Lord Colwyn in May 1924. The ground was laid on the bed of the old Conway river, although locals say it was probably a large ditch or swamp. The Penrhyn Avenue ground is square in shape and little has changed since 1924 other than the introduction of some banking at the southern end for deck chairs. Ground improvements in 1950 cost £4,000 and in 1969 the old pavilion was demolished and the new existing structure was built. The pavilion offers excellent facilities and a glance at the record board in the Long Room will show that the club has supported many charity raising events over the years including the Prisoners of War Fund and the Liverpool Air Raid Disaster Fund. The largest crowd for a first-class match was 6,000 for the visit

of Derbyshire in 1966. This picture shows an aerial view of the ground in 1934. *Aerofilms*

Below right:
The best bowling performance in an innings for Glamorgan in a first-class match at Colwyn Bay is 9 for 49 by A. E. Cordle versus Leicestershire in 1969. *Authors collection*

COLWYN BAY

Sophia Gardens during a Benson & Hedges Cup match between Glamorgan and Kent, 1989

Inset:

The first matches staged by Glamorgan CCC in Cardiff were at the Arms Park ground, adjoining the National Stadium. Glamorgan moved to its present home, Sophia Gardens, during the winter of 1966-67 ready for the 1967 season. Approximately 10.5 acres of ground were used for cricket, the remainder was built on in 1970-71 when the Cardiff Corporation offered land to the Sports Council so that the National Sports Centre for Wales could be constructed. The ground is also used by Cardiff Cricket Club, which first played at Sophia Gardens in 1966. Glamorgan's first home match at Sophia Gardens in 1967 was against the Indian tourists and the first County Championship match was against Northamptonshire.

The ground at Sophia Gardens - originally pleasure gardens - is located very close to the River Taff and takes its name from Sophia, the second wife of the Second Marquess of Bute. The ground was originally part of the Bute estate which stretched from the city centre north along both banks of the River Taff and close to Cardiff castle. With a 99 year lease on the ground Cardiff Athletic Club built a new pavilion, offices and a scoreboard in 1966-67, the latter thanks to a donation from London Welsh sportsman Sir Edward Lewis. This picture shows an aerial view of the ground in 1947 before the move from the Arms Park. *Aerofilms*

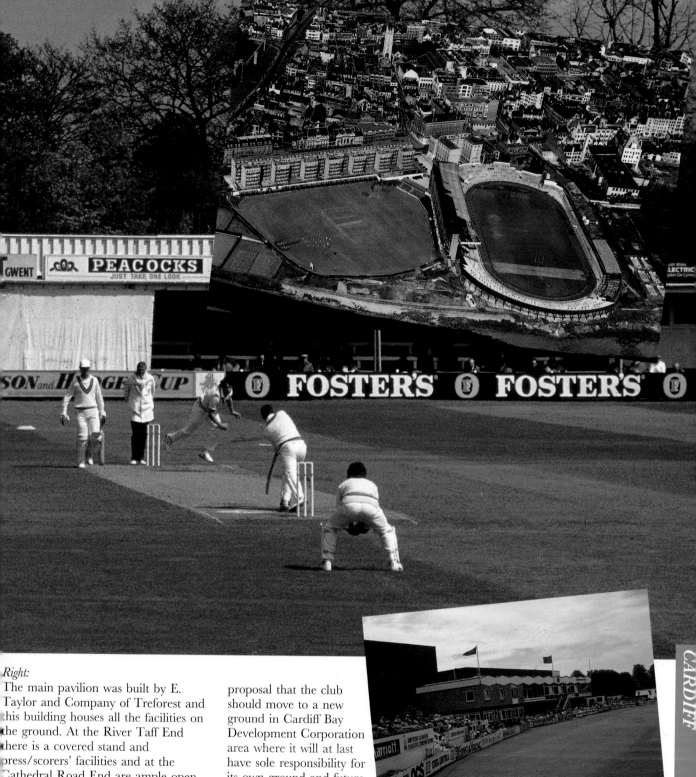

Right:

The main pavilion was built by E. Taylor and Company of Treforest and this building houses all the facilities on the ground. At the River Taff End there is a covered stand and press/scorers' facilities and at the Cathedral Road End are ample open terrace seating areas. Wilfred Wooller, the former Glamorgan player, commented that Sophia Gardens is 'a quite delightful rural setting, spacious and well-treed but somehow it has never reproduced the cosy atmosphere at Cardiff Arms Park'. There is a proposal that the club should move to a new ground in Cardiff Bay Development Corporation area where it will at last have sole responsibility for its own ground and future.

Many notable matches have been staged at Sophia Gardens including that in 1969 when Glamorgan won the County Championship. That day Glamorgan beat neighbours Worcestershire in front of some 16,000 people, still a record attendance for the ground.

This view of the pavilion was taken in 1993. *Author*

Below:

Neath Cricket Club was founded in 1848 and its home ground is situated at the Gnoll close to the better-known home of Neath RFC. Glamorgan's Indoor Cricket School is also sited at the club. Behind the pavilion is the high wooded slope from which the ground gets its name. At the top was once to be found Gnoll House, the former home of Sir Humphrey Mackworth who owned much of the land. In 1934 Glamorgan played its initial first-class County Championship match at Neath against Essex. In 1923 Gnoll House and the estate were acquired by the Neath Corporation from the Evan Thomas family as a war memorial and to provide recreational and sporting facilities for the residents of the town. During World War 2 the Gnoll sustained some damage and in 1947 the county club gave Neath Council £300 towards repairing the cricket arena. In 1948 cricket returned and in 1950 Glamorgan CCC decided to establish an indoor cricket school, which was opened by R. E. S. Wyatt in 1954. More recently, after modernisation and refurbishment, it was reopened by the late C. F. Walters in 1984. Some 12,000 watched the Warwickshire County Championship match in 1948 and in 1985, after an absence of 11 seasons, Glamorgan CCC returned to the Gnoll, thanks to sponsorship from the Neath Borough Council, to stage the tour match with the Australians; this same fixture has followed in 1989 and 1993. This picture shows an aerial view of Neath in 1929. *Aerofilms*

Below right:

The highest individual innings for Glamorgan in a first-class match at Neath is 200 no by Pakistani Javed Miandad against the touring Australian in 1985. *County Print Services*

JAVED MIANDAD

NEATH

50

Above:

Located within Ynysangharad Park is the home ground of Pontypridd Cricket Club established in 1870. The ground is also the town's war memorial and is located on a flat area of land on the eastern side of the River Taff between the river and the main A470 trunk road. The parkland in which the ground stands was originally given to the town by the Lenox family as a memorial to the soldiers and servicemen from the Welsh town who died during World War 1. The park was opened in 1923 by Field Marshall Lord Allenby and in 1924-30 was also used by Pontypridd Rugby Football Club until they moved to another ground in the town during the late 1970s. Glamorgan CCC first visited Pontypridd in 1926 when Derbyshire provided the opposition and during the late 1920s matches were staged annually; these included a tour match with the South Africans in 1929. Over the years the ground has had significant problems with rain and the majority of Glamorgan's matches so affected appear to be at Pontypridd. This was commented upon in the 1947 Glamorgan County Cricket Club Review: 'Pontypridd appears to be Glamorgan's most unlucky ground as rain interferes with the majority of matches played there'. The largest crowd at Pontypridd was in 1933 when 6,000 were present for the visit of neighbours Gloucestershire. This picture shows an aerial view of Pontypridd in 1932. *Aerofilms*

Right:

The best bowling performance against Glamorgan in a first-class match at Pontypridd is 16 for 96 by George Geary of Leicestershire in 1929. *Author's collection*

G. GEARY, LEICESTER

Above:

Glamorgan CCC first played at the St Helen's Ground in 1921 when Leicestershire visited. The ground was originally owned by an order of Augustinian nuns who built a convent dedicated to St Helen but following the dissolution of the monasteries it passed to Baron Herbert of Cardiff and the Earl of Pembroke and subsequently to Colonel Llewellyn Morgan, a major landowner in Swansea. Swansea Cricket Club was established in 1850 and international rugby matches were staged on the ground from 1882 - when Wales played England - until shortly after World War 2. In 1939 St Helen's was sold to the Swansea Town Corporation, now the City Corporation, which remains the sole owner.

During World War 2 the ground was used as a military training camp; since then, much rebuilding has taken place including a new rugby grandstand, new terracing and improved pavilion facilities. This aerial picture shows St Helen's in 1958. The pavilion was built in 1927 and has had various extensions, additions and refurbishments, most recently in 1980 when a new eastern wing was constructed. There used to be 67 steps down to the playing area from the players' pavilion - a very long walk for a batsman who had been dismissed cheaply - but during the 1980s the distance was reduced to 45 steps. In 1959 the Memorial Gates donated by the Swansea and District RSC. were installed opposite the Cricketers Inn in memory of past players who have represented Swansea Cricket and Football Clubs. Since this picture taken in 1964, four 140ft-high floodlight pylons have been installed at each corner which dominate the ground.

Many of Glamorgan's finest hours have come at St Helen's including a victory over the Australians by 36 runs in 1964 when the attendance was 50,000. This remains a record as the present ground capacity is only 20,000. Two of the most significant cricket records also took place at St Helen's. In 1968, while batting for Nottinghamshire, Gary Sobers hit Glamorgan's Malcolm Nash for 36 runs in a single six-ball over and in 1990 Tom Moody, playing for Warwickshire, scored the fastest century in first-class cricket off 36 balls in only 26 minutes to break the record of 37 minutes held jointly by P. G. H. Fender and S. O'Shaughnessy. *Aerofilms*

Inset:

The highest individual innings in a first-class match at Swansea is 257 by A. H. Bakewell for Northamptonshire versus Glamorgan in 1933. *County Print Services*

Gloucestershire

GLOUCESTERSHIRE

Above:
The present ground, first used by Gloucestershire CCC in its match against Lancashire in 1899, was laid out to W. G. Grace's specifications. In 1916 the ground was sold to Fry's Chocolate Company to ease the county's debts and became known as The Fry's Ground. This picture shows the ground in 1907. *Author's collection*

Left:
From 1840 to 1870 the ground was used by Muller's Orphanage. The orphanage building still exists and now forms part of the Bristol University campus. The main entrance to the ground from Nevil Road is through the Grace Gates and a tablet depicting Dr W. G. Grace was erected on 18 July 1948 - the centenary of his birth. As John Arlott wrote: 'in the public mind W. G. was Gloucestershire'. This picture shows a view of the tablet. *Author*

Top:
The club badge of Gloucestershire CCC. *County Print Services*

53

Below:

The county repurchased the ground in 1932 after forming the Gloucestershire CCC Limited Company but because of financial problems sold it again in 1976 to the Phoenix Assurance Company, when it was renamed The Phoenix Assurance County Ground. The pavilion was built during the 1880s but has been added to in recent years. The Jessop Tavern which also houses the press box was built in 1958, the nearby scoreboard was constructed in 1971 and the Mound Stand was built during the 1960s. The Grace Room and Hammond Room, at the Pavilion End, now form the main members' restaurant. This picture shows an aerial view taken in 1920. *Aerofilms*

Right:

Many changes have taken place since W. G. Grace first contemplated the development of the County Ground a century ago but it retains a sense of spaciousness. It now houses facilities for indoor cricket nets, squash courts, tennis and even an outdoor golf driving range as well as football and hockey pitches during the winter months. Further ground improvements took place during the winters of 1991-92 and 1992-93, including a new indoor cricket school and the replacement of the wooden seating with plastic tip-up seats. This recent development confirms that the county's headquarters will remain at Bristol for the foreseeable future (although at one time members thought it should be at Gloucester).

The best crowds at Bristol were 15,000 for the visits of the touring Australians in 1930 and 1948. This 198[?] picture shows the pavilion before rebuilding in 1992. *Author*

Above:
Gloucestershire CCC have staged a cricket festival at the Cheltenham College Ground since their initial first-class match against Surrey in July 1872. The first visits to Cheltenham College were organised by James Lillywhite, the former Sussex player. He died in 1882 never knowing the full success of his venture. This 1935 picture shows an aerial view of the ground and its permanent buildings.

The main permanent building used by the county club during matches is the gymnasium with its twin steeples of yellow brick and its trellised balcony. This is used as a members' pavilion and for the players' dressing rooms. Other buildings on this side of the playing area are smaller pavilions for schoolboy cricket, used during term time only. The largest crowd on the ground was 15,000 for the match against Middlesex in 1947. *Aerofilms*

Right:
The best bowling performance in an innings in a first-class match at Cheltenham College is 10 for 66 by A. A. Mailey for the touring Australians versus Gloucestershire in 1921. *Author's collection*

A. A. MAILEY

The temporary stands on the Thirlestaine
Road side of the ground, as well as many
marquees and tents, are provided during
festival weeks. The college chapel which
overlooks the ground was built in 1893.
This 1988 picture shows a game in progress
with the college buildings in the
background. *Author*

Inset:
The highest individual innings in a first-class
match at Cheltenham College is 318 no by
Dr W. G. Grace for Gloucestershire versus
Yorkshire in 1876.

Left:
Gloucestershire CCC have played at Tuffley Avenue since their first first-class match on the ground against Lancashire in June 1923. Since that initial visit the ground has had various names: for its first 102 years it was known as the Gloucestershire Railway Carriage and Wagon Company Ground until in 1962 it was taken over by the Gloucester Engineering Sports Club and, shortly afterwards, by the Babcocks and Wilcox Sports Club. Today the ground is called Winget Sports Ground and is used by Winget Cricket Club. This picture shows an aerial view of the ground in 1926. Aerofilms

Above:
The original 33-acre ground was bought by the railway carriage company from the executors of a Colonel Collett in 1917 for £4,005.

Approximately 20 acres were sold off for £525,000 in 1973 to a house builder; the remainder forms the cricket ground, which is situated in a residential area to the south of Gloucester city centre. There were 12 plane trees in front of the pavilion but upon the death of a prominent club member one tree was felled.

In recent years the ground has again changed hands and is now owned by Gloucester City Council who acquired it for £75,000 - a nominal price for the 13 remaining acres - saving the ground laid out by G. L. Jessop during the winter of 1917-18 from further housing development. This picture shows a view of play in progress in 1988. The best attendance was 9,000 for the visit of Surrey in 1959. *Author*

Above right:
The best bowling performance in a first-class match at Tuffley Park is 15 for 56 by C. W. L. Parker for Gloucestershire versus Essex in 1925. *Author's collection*

Above:
Gloucestershire made their debut at
King's School, Archdeacon Meadow,
Gloucester in 1993 when they switched
the four day County Championship
match against neighbours
Worcestershire from Tuffley Avenue,
Gloucester, as the wicket was not fit for
first-class cricket. King's School, located
close to the city centre, was the third
ground to have been used in the city by
Gloucestershire; the others being the
Spa Ground used from 1882 to 1923
and Tuffley Avenue from 1923 to 1992.
This aerial view of the ground in 1991
shows its close proximity to the
cathedral, city centre and railway line.
Aerofilms

Right:
Play in progress at Archdeacon
Meadow during the initial first-class
match in 1993, with the pavilion and
cathedral in the background. *Author*

Hampshire

HAMPSHIRE

Above:

The County Cricket Ground at Northlands Road was opened in May 1885 by the Countess of Northesk, wife of the then club president. The ground was leased for an annual payment of £160 on the condition that a pavilion be built. This was done and £2,000 was raised before the opening match between North and South Hampshire. The initial first-class match was with the MCC in 1885 and the first County Championship match was against Derbyshire in the same season. In 1893 the Hampshire County Ground Company was founded and bought the freehold of the ground from Sir Edward Hulse for £5,400. In 1896 the present pavilion frontage and an adjacent ladies' pavilion were built. Further building took place in 1900 and 1911: the football stand was redeveloped and a scoreboard built opposite the members' pavilion. The ground has also been used for hockey and at the City End (formerly the Bannister Park End) was Bannister Park Speedway Stadium. This has now been replaced by housing. Facilities for tennis and bowling are still available behind the indoor cricket school built in 1958. This picture shows the ground in 1988.
Author

Right:
The best bowling performance recorded in a first-class match at Southampton is 17 for 119 by W. Mead for Essex versus Hampshire in 1900.
Author's collection

Top:
The club badge of Hampshire CCC.
County Print Services

Above:

The largest attendance for a first-class match at Southampton was 15,000 for the visit of the Australians in 1938. After World War 2 donations were invited for ground improvements at but the £10,927 raised was insufficient to carry out all the work envisaged. The 1960s saw the link between the two pavilions built and the bell installed from the old Cunard liner Athlone Castle. There was no further major development until the improvements to the indoor cricket school, with the opening of the Hampshire Squash and Sports Club in April 1983. On the first floor is the Desmond Eagar Room which contains the hospitality suites used during county matches. The most recent addition is the Philip Mead

Stand built in 1986, close to the club offices and next to the cricket nets, which provides hospitality boxes for executive members. It is said the ground is now worth several million pounds and the club is planning to move from Northlands Road to a new greenfield site to the east of the city centre. This picture shows an aerial view of the ground in 1938. *Aerofilms*

Right:
The highest individual innings in a first-class match at Southampton is 292 by L. C. H. Palairet for Somerset versus Hampshire in 1896. *County Print Services*

L. C. H. PALAIRET

Below:
The United Services Officers Sports Ground is an historic venue. Situated in Burnaby Road it is used for Services matches, including matches with touring sides, and is now the only military ground used for first-class cricket. The county's link with the United Services Ground began in 1888 when they played Sussex. They did not use the ground again until they attained first-class status in 1895 when a solitary match was staged with Leicestershire. The railway between the Portsmouth & Southsea and Portsmouth Harbour Stations runs behind the pavilion and across the road. At the other end of the ground the Portsmouth University buildings dominate the enclosed playing area, as does the US Officers' club which was built in 1950 as a recreational and residential centre for Services sport, principally for the Royal Navy. This picture shows an aerial view of the ground in 1951. *Aerofilms*

Below right:
The initial first-class match was staged in 1882 when the Australians played Cambridge Past and Present. In the following year the Australians scored 843 against Cambridge and Oxford Past and Present; the innings lasted into a third day which was a record for first-class cricket at the time and remains the highest score made by an Australian team in this country. The scorecard of this match is displayed in the pavilion. The highest attendance of 10,000 was for the County Championship match with Sussex in 1948. This picture shows the pavilion in 1991. *Author*

Inset:
The highest individual innings in a first-class match at Portsmouth is 302 no by Percy Holmes for Yorkshire versus Hampshire in 1920. *Author's collection*

HOLMES

Above:

May's Bounty Ground is the home of the Basingstoke and North Hants Cricket Club, founded in 1865. It was created by John May as club president after the Gents of Basingstoke Cricket Club was disbanded in 1864, 24 years after it was formed. Cricket has been played in the town since 1817, but the ground was first used for cricket in 1855 and it continues to be played there to this day. In 1880 John May purchased the land to prevent building taking place on the ground and in 1885 the Basingstoke Athletic Club was formed with cricket, football and cycling sections. In 1901 the club's title was changed to its present name. The ground was bought in 1950 for £450 freehold and the club became the proprietor of one of the finest grounds in the county for an absurdly low price. This picture shows an aerial view of the ground in 1920. *Aerofilms*

Above right:

The original pavilion was built in 1877 and was a single-storey thatched building. It was replaced in 1901 by the present building, with additions in 1965. Two squash courts were added in 1974, a further club room and kitchen in 1979 and in 1986 a third squash court, committee/snooker room and general club office were built. This picture shows the pavilion in 1994. Hampshire CCC first staged a match at May's Bounty in 1906 when Warwickshire visited. The late John Arlott, who was born in Basingstoke, witnessed his first cricket match at May's Bounty and in 1938 played his only game for the club there. Crowds are always very good and the 5,000 crowd for the 1986 County Championship match against Surrey was one of the largest. Author

Kent

Above:

Originally the ground formed part of the Winter's Farm Estate, Nackington. It was bought from the landlord, Lord Sondes, for £4,500 in 1896. The first match of importance staged on the ground was in early August 1847 when Kent played an England XI and won by 3 wickets. A Canterbury cricket festival is always staged in early August, the first was organized in 1848. The headquarters of Kent CCC, the St Lawrence Cricket Ground in Old Dover Road was opened in 1847. At that time it was known as the Beverley Cricket Ground - the present name originates from the adjoining St Lawrence House which was originally the St Lawrence priory, founded in 1137. It is the only cricket ground in the county solely owned by Kent CCC. This picture shows an aerial view of the ground in 1930. *Aerofilms*

Left:
A view of the memorial to Colin Blythe who died in 1917, located close to the main entrance off Old Dover Road. *Author*

Top:
The club badge of Kent CCC. *County Print Services*

65

Below

The main pavilion was built in 1900 at a cost of £2,340. In 1970 it was refurbished, enlarged and renamed the Stuart Chiesman Pavilion following the club's centenary appeal. The Iron Stand was constructed in 1897 and renamed the Leslie Ames Stand in 1973. It now accommodates sixteen executive boxes and a new enlarged scoreboard. The concrete stand was built in the winter of 1926-27 and renamed the Frank Woolley Stand. This is an aerial view of the ground in 1988 during the festival week. *Kent Messenger*

Right:

The Howard Levett Kent Indoor Cricket School was demolished in the winter of 1990-91 and replaced during the winter of 1991-92 by the Ames Levett Indoor Cricket School, built by Abbott Construction. It includes cricket nets, changing facilities and hospitality suites for county matches. A lime tree stands within the playing area on the Old Dover Road side of the ground and was once cleared by a hit from Learie Constantine and, more recently, by Carl Hooper in 1992. These two West Indians are the only players to accomplish this feat.
The most recent addition is the New Stand, comprising two levels, which was built in 1986 at a cost of £600,000. The Kent CCC Souvenir Shop and scorecards sales point are at the rear and a public bar and fast food restaurant are on the ground floor. A dining room is also available for members and the top floor houses the Kent CCC Executive Club and suite. The majority of funds to build the New Stand came from the Kent CCC Project '85 appeal. This 1986 picture shows the pavilion, annexe, New Stand and Frank Woolley Stand. *Author*

Above:
The first Kent CCC match at Mote Park was in June 1859 when an MCC team visited but it was not until 1870 that Kent began to play regularly at the county town of Maidstone. Mote Park is attractively located within the 558-acre Mote Estate which lies to the east of the town centre. The park dates back to the 13th century and contains the late-18th-century Mote House, now a Cheshire Home. The ground dates from the formation of the Mote Cricket Club in 1857, one of the oldest clubs in the county. Sir Marcus Sammel, later the First Viscount Bearstead, the last private owner of the Mote Estate, was responsible in 1908 for levelling the playing area. At that time the wicket was moved 90 degrees to its present layout. The pavilion, which has two levels, is one of the most attractive at a county out ground. This picture shows an aerial view of the ground taken in 1930. *Aerofilms*

Right:
The highest individual innings in a first-class match at Maidstone is 260 by Percy Chapman for Kent versus Lancashire in 1927. *Author's collection*

20. A. P. F. CHAPMAN

Far right:
The main pavilion was constructed during the winter of 1909-10 and this 1986 picture shows it and the smaller pavilion, known as the Tabernacle. The latter is one of cricket's architectural curiosities and was originally Viscount Bearstead's private pavilion. After his death the Second Viscount Bearstead sold the estate in 1928 to its present owner, the Maidstone Borough Council, but the cricket ground was reserved and presented to Mote CC. *Author*

Above:
The main permanent buildings on the ground with play in progress in 1988. The best crowd to attend a County Championship match at Mote Park was 8,000 for the visit of Essex in 1948. *Author*

Right:
The best bowling performance recorded in a first-class match is 15 for 117 by D. J. Halfyard for Kent versus Worcestershire in 1959. *Author's collection*

Royal Tunbridge Wells from Forest Road.

158.

V. W. C. JUPP

59·C NORTHAMPTONSHIRE

Above:
The Nevill Ground is one of the most beautiful grounds on the county circuit, especially during Tunbridge Wells festival week, usually staged in early June, when the giant purple blooms of the rhododendron bushes around the playing arena form a superb setting. The ground is located at Nevill Gate and is the home of Tunbridge Wells Cricket Club, established in 1762, and the Blue Mantles Cricket Club, established in 1895. This picture shows a view of the ground in 1913 taken from the slope high above the Pavilion End.
Author's collection

Far right:
Tunbridge Wells Cricket, Football and Athletic Club acquired the ground on a lease of 99 years from the Eridge Park Estate of the Marquess of Abergavenny (family name Nevill). It has been used for football, cycle racing, athletics, archery, hockey and lawn tennis. The ground was opened in 1898 by the Marquess of Abergavenny and the first Kent CCC first-class match was staged in 1901 against Lancashire. This 1937 picture shows an aerial view of the ground, laid out ready for the festival week. *Aerofilms*

Right:
The best bowling performance in an innings in a first-class match at Tunbridge Wells is 10 for 127 by V. W. C. Jupp for Northamptonshire versus Kent in 1932. *Author's collection*

JAMES SEYMOUR,

KENT.

Top left:
The present pavilion and additional buildings were constructed in 1903 at a cost of £1,200 and this picture shows a view of the pavilion with play in progress in 1926. *Ron Harries*

Above:
In 1913 the Nevill Ground suffered extensive fire damage during the suffragettes' campaign; the pavilion was rebuilt shortly afterwards. During World War 1 the ground became a picketing area for the cavalry; several hundred horses were tethered on it and did little to improve the playing area and the wicket! From 1946 the ground has been owned and maintained by the Tunbridge Wells Borough Council. This picture shows play in progress in 1988. The largest crowd at the Nevill Ground was in 1950 when 10,000 attended the two days of the County Championship with Lancashire. *Author*

Top Right
The highest individual innings in a first-class match for Kent at Tunbridge Wells is 214 by J. Seymour versus Essex in 1914. *Author's collection*

Lancashire

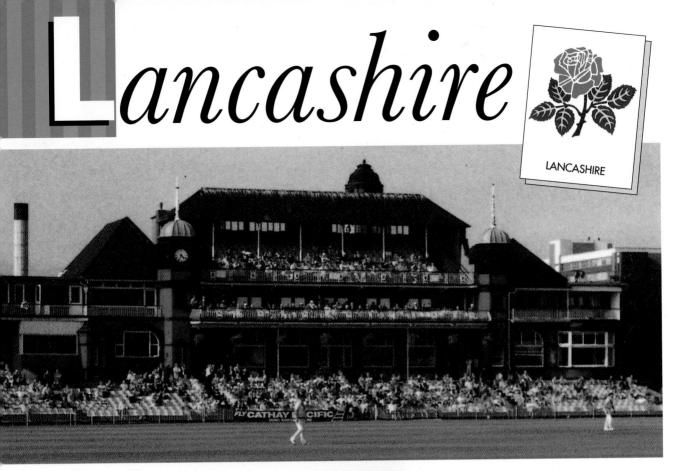

LANCASHIRE

Left:
Old Trafford has been the headquarters of Lancashire CCC since 1857 when the new cricket ground was opened. This aerial picture of the ground and surrounding area was taken during the England versus Australia Test Match of 1961 and shows the large adjacent car parking areas before the construction of the government office towers on them. The buildings in Talbot Road are named after famous Lancashire cricketers from the past: Statham, MacLaren, Duckworth and Washbrook. A garden centre and DIY warehouse were built in subsequent years at the Stretford End of the ground. *Airviews Manchester Airport*

Above:
The pavilion, seen here in 1988, was designed by the architect Mr A. T. Muirhead - also responsible for the design of the Oval pavilion at Kennington in London. *Author's collection*

Top:
The club badge of Lancashire CCC. *County Print Services*

73

R. B. Simpson
Australia

Right:
The 18-acre ground was owned by Sir Thomas de Trafford until Manchester CC purchased it from the de Trafford estate for £24,082 in 1898. The main pavilion was built four years earlier and was used as a hospital during World War 1; it was bombed during World War 2 but was later repaired. The majority of the permanent buildings are on the Talbot Road side of the ground and all the seating is permanent.

The ground is situated within the Old Trafford district of Manchester to the south of the city centre. It is bounded by Talbot Road to the north, Sir Matt Busby Way to the north-east, Great Stone Road to the west and the Altrincham to Manchester tram line to the south. This aerial view was taken in 1928 with a match in progress watched by a capacity crowd. *Aerofilms*

Above:
The highest individual innings in a first-class match at Old Trafford is 311 by Bobby Simpson for Australia versus England during the 1964 Test Match.
County Print Services

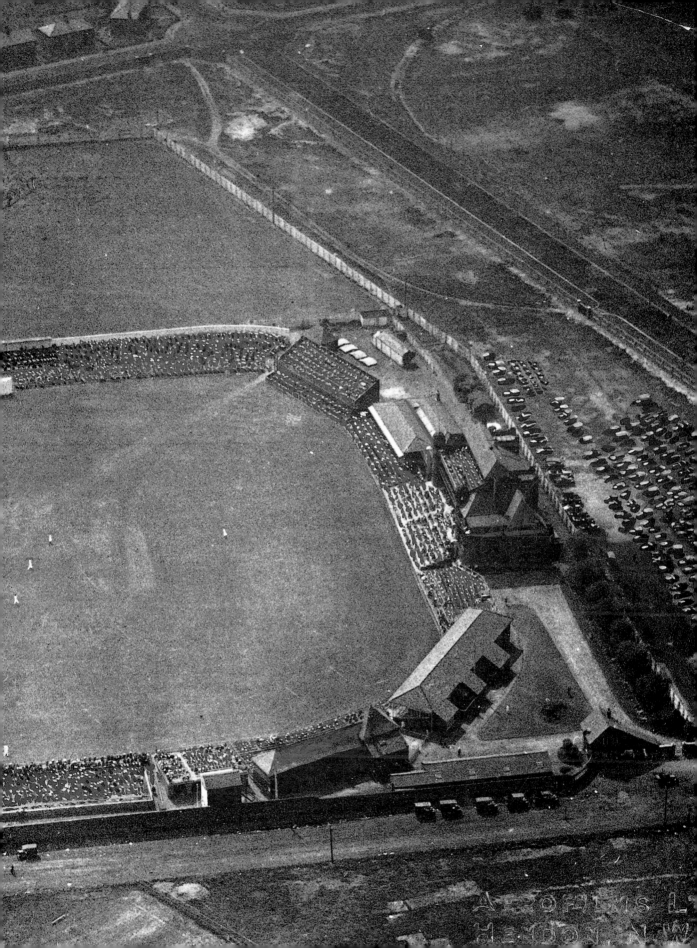

AEROFILMS L
HENDON N.W.

Right:

The majority of seating is now of the blue plastic tip-up type. During the season of 1982 a ground development appeal raised £200,000 and in 1984 a further £47,000 was raised from a Test centenary appeal. These funds have been used to improve facilities for spectators. This picture shows a china plate produced by the club to celebrate the centenary of Test cricket at Old Trafford in 1984. *Author*

Above:

Much development has taken place using the funds from these two appeals, including the construction of some executive boxes at the Stretford End, the building of the Red Rose Suite and improved press/commentary facilities at the City End. The press box is known as the Sir Neville Cardus Gallery and was opened by John Arlott on the eve of the Test Match between England and Pakistan on 3 June 1987. Other recent improvements have included an improved and enlarged Lancashire CCC museum and a members' library in the pavilion. This aerial picture of the ground was taken in 1991 during the England versus West Indies one-day international match and shows the new development at both ends of the ground. *Jefferson Air Photography*

Right:
There are a number of interesting items in the pavilion including, in this picture, the LCCC bell which is sounded to inform the players that they have five minutes to take the field before play commences. *Author*

Below:
This 1993 picture shows the new Wilson Stand built during the winter of 1992-93 by Shepherd Construction of York and opened before the one-day international match between England and Australia in 1993. It is a two-tier stand and although the top deck has no cover for spectators the two weather vanes remain sited at either end of the stand at a similar level to those on the original Wilson Stand. The record attendance at Old Trafford for a first-class match is 78,617 for the Lancashire versus Yorkshire Roses Match of 1926 with some 46,000 attending the first day. *Author*

Left:
The initial first-class match staged at Blackpool was in 1905 when the North played the South. However, Lancashire CCC first staged a match on the present ground in 1904 against an England XI. In order to prolong the match, the laws of cricket were not adhered to in the later stages and the match was ruled not to be first-class. This aerial picture of the ground was taken in 1948. *Aerofilms*

Below:
The present home ground of Blackpool Cricket Club is at Stanley Park. Formerly named Whitegate Park, it was donated to the club in 1924 by Sir Lindsay Parkinson who stated that the ground should be owned by trustees comprising one member of Blackpool CC and either himself or another

member of his family. Another condition was that the club should erect a stand for spectators and the present pavilion was built the following year. The ground covers four acres and is enclosed in the park - a long walk from the popular seafront and the holiday residential areas. In 1957 an additional stand was built, costing £6,000, together with a new scoreboard and groundsman's store. Many of the permanent buildings on the ground have been dedicated to officials. These include the members' seating adjoining the pavilion - 'dedicated to Winnie and Fred Dawson for their lifetime work for the club' and the scoreboard - 'thanks to donations from Mr W. B. Corry' in 1954 and in 'memory of past chairman Mr J. Holden - funds raised by the ladies committee' in 1979. This picture

of the ground and pavilion shows a league match in progress between Blackpool and Preston in 1988. The ground attendances at Blackpool are usually very good during the holiday period of July and August and the best was 13,872 for the County Championship match versus Glamorgan in 1950. *Author*

Below right:
The best bowling performance recorded in a first-class match at Blackpool is 15 for 95 by C. H. Parkin for Lancashire versus Glamorgan in 1923. *Author's collection*

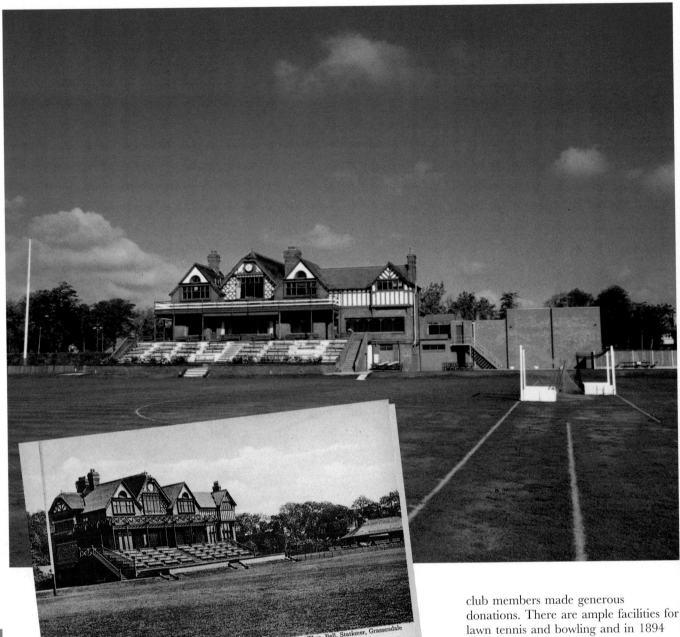

The Pavilion, Liverpool Cricket Ground, Aigburth

Thos. Bell, Stationer, Grassendale

Above:
Lancashire CCC first staged a match at Liverpool in 1881 when Cambridge University visited the Aigburth Cricket Ground located in the Aigburth district of the city, five miles from the Liver Building. The Liverpool Cricket Club was founded in 1807, in the days of the Mosslake Cricket Society, and established its headquarters at Aigburth in 1881. This picture shows the pavilion in 1920. *Author's collection*

Right:
The ground is located at the corner of Aigburth Road and Riverside Road which leads down to the River Mersey. The pavilion was constructed in 1880 by the building contractor Cubitts and is situated at the Aigburth Road End of the ground. It is very grand for an out ground with distinctive green and white painted weather-boarding. During the 1880s, when the ground was built, Liverpool was a thriving port and the

club members made generous donations. There are ample facilities for lawn tennis and bowling and in 1894 the Northern Lawn Tennis Association Tournament was staged on the ground. This aerial picture was taken in 1963. *Aerofilms*

Top:
The largest attendance for a first-class match at Liverpool was 15,164 for the visit of Northamptonshire in 1948. The Aigburth pavilion boasts one of the largest players' dressing rooms on the county circuit, larger than at most Test venues. This picture shows a view of the pavilion and ground in 1986. *Author*

Right:
The first Lancashire
CCC visit to Southport
was in 1959 for a
County Championship match against
Worcestershire. The home of the
Southport and Birkdale Cricket Club,
established in 1859, the ground is
located in Trafalgar Road. It was
purchased in 1884 with agreement from
the Weld-Blundell family and the
Birkdale Park Land Company, when
the Birkdale Cricket Ground Company
was established. Birkdale CC was
established in 1874 and merged with
Southport CC in 1901 to form the new
club.

Originally, the ground was an area
of waste and sand hills to the south of
the Southport to Liverpool railway line
but in 1850 it was developed by a Mr
J. Aughton, an enterprising building
contractor from Preston. In 1881 the
present pavilion was erected for
approximately £300; it was rebuilt in
1965 as the facilities were no longer
satisfactory to club members, nor
adequate for Lancashire CCC's annual
visit. This aerial picture of the ground
shows the pavilions and the nearby
railway line in 1962. The Ladies'
Pavilion was erected in 1958 together
with a bowling green and the new
players' pavilion was constructed in
1965 at a cost of £28,000 and opened
by Lord Derby. The best attendance
for a first-class match at Southport was
4,500 for the game versus
Worcestershire in 1959. *Aerofilms*

Above:
The highest individual innings in a first-
class match at Southport is 254 by
Geoff Humpage for Warwickshire
versus Lancashire in 1982.
Warwickshire CCC

Top:

Lancashire CCC made their initial first-class visit to Church Road, Lytham in 1985 for a County Championship match versus Northamptonshire which was affected by rain. Taking an annual match to the Fylde coast resort, usually in August, the county club tend to attract a bumper crowd of holiday makers for a day or so away from the sandy beaches. The home of the Lytham Cricket and Sports Club, the ground comprises a pleasant grassed area of 11.25 acres nestling in trees close to the Preston-Blackpool South railway line which passes through a cutting at its northern end. This aerial view was taken in 1946. *Aerofilms*

Above left:

The only permanent buildings on the ground are the players' pavilion and clubhouse located on the side closest to the parish hall and St Cuthbert's Church. An interesting old scoreboard is located under the trees near the tennis courts and this is shown in this picture. The majority of facilities for county matches are temporary and include raised open seating at the Church Road End. The largest crowd for a single day at Lytham was 3,500 for Glamorgan's visit in 1986 and, over the three days, 6,750 for the visit of Sussex in 1987. *Author*

The highest individual innings in a first-class match at Lytham is 171 by John Stephenson for Essex versus Lancashire in 1991. *Essex CCC*

Leicestershire

Left:
In 1877 the Leicestershire Cricket Ground Company purchased 16 acres of land to the south of the city centre, bordered by Grace, Milligan and Hawkesbury Roads. The first cricket match took place there the following year but the initial first-class match did not follow until 1894 when Yorkshire visited. Leicestershire used the Grace Road ground for County Championship cricket from 1895, but after five years it was decided that a ground was needed closer to the city centre. This picture shows an aerial view of Grace Road in 1969. *Aerofilms*

Above:
The Meet, Butler Stand, Fernie Suite, Main Pavilion and Quorn Suite seen from under the trees on the Park Hill Drive side of the ground in 1993. *Author*

Top:
The club badge of Leicestershire CCC. *County Print Services*

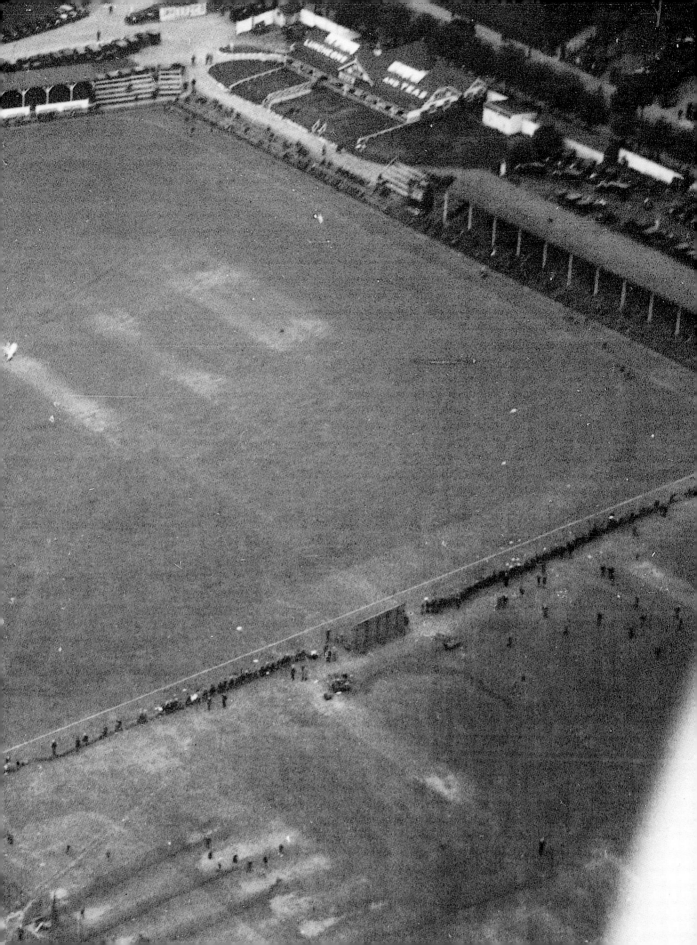

Back Row : Mr. A. James (Masseur), Mr. W. J. Dowling (Manager), K. Mackay, J. W. Burke, J. Rutherford, A. K. Davidson, P. Burge, P. Crawford, R. Benaud, R. G. Archer, C. C. McDonald, Mr. W. L. Rush (Assistant-Manager), Mr. N. Gorman (Scorer)
Middle Row : I. D. Craig, R. N. Harvey, K. R. Miller, I. W. Johnson (Captain), R. R. Lindwall, G. R. Langley
In Front : L. Maddocks, J. Wilson

AUSTRALIAN CRICKET TEAM, 1956

Previous page:
Leicestershire CCC moved from Grace Road to Aylestone Road at the start of the 1901 season and remained there until 1939; during World War 2 the ground was damaged and partly used for industrial development. A return to Grace Road was suggested and the county returned to the ground they had left 46 years earlier. This picture shows an aerial view of Aylestone Road in 1927 with the players taking the field after tea. *Aerofilms*

Above:
Obtaining the use of Grace Road from the local education authority, the county club brought with them from Aylestone Road the stand known as the 'Meet' (seen in the corner of Picture 2) and also a heavy roller. In 1966 the Grace Road ground was purchased and was considerably developed in the 1970s and 1980s with the erection of new dressing rooms, stands with plastic tip-up seats, an indoor cricket school, executive suites and a modern scoreboard. Grace Road is one of the best equipped grounds on the county circuit outside the six main Test Match venues. The record attendance for a first-class match is 16,000 in 1948

against the touring Australians.
Thanks to a substantial donation from Mr Trevor Bennett, a local businessman, a new stand and leisure complex has been constructed at the Bennett End - formerly known as the Hawkesbury Road End - of the ground and was opened in 1993. This picture shows a view of the new complex in 1993. *Author*

Above right:
The George Geary Stand and new scoreboard in 1994. *Author*

Inset:
The highest first-class innings total at Grace Road of 694 for 6 declared was recorded by the touring Australians versus Leicestershire in 1956. *Author*

Middlesex

MIDDLESEX

Lord's during the 1991 Test Match against the West Indies. *Author*

Left:
Established in 1789, the Uxbridge Cricket Club claims to be the oldest club in Middlesex, although its ground at Park Road was only inaugurated in 1971. Middlesex CCC were first approached to play a match at Uxbridge in 1979 but this Prudential Cup warm-up match was cancelled due to poor weather and it was not until August in the following summer that Middlesex played their initial first-class game at Uxbridge, defeating Derbyshire by 10 wickets. This picture shows the old cricket ground in Cricket Field Lane, Uxbridge, where the London borough of Hillingdon council offices are now situated, and the present ground at Park Road. These are depicted on a china plate issued by the club for the bicentenary in 1989 showing the ground then and now.
Author

Top:
The club badge of Middlesex CCC.
County Print Services

D. L. HAYNES

Left:
The highest individual innings in a first-class match at Uxbridge is 206 no by West Indian Desmond Haynes for Middlesex versus Kent in 1989.
County Print Services

Above and left:
The ground is part of a large sports complex providing facilities for squas football, tennis and bowls as well as swimming pool and a dry ski-slope. pavilion has been extended since it v constructed during the winter of 197 71 and now includes squash courts a an additional members' bar which is used as a players' dining area during county matches. The County Bar an viewing area were opened in 1981 b the former Middlesex and England s bowler Phil Edmonds. These picture show the ground in 1993. The highe attendance for a match at Uxbridge was in 1991 when an exhibition gam between India and Pakistan attracted crowd of 6,500 although it had to be abandoned when the crowd invaded the pitch. Middlesex's best attendanc for a first-class match at Park Road v 4,500 for the visit of Gloucestershire 1988. *Author*

Below:

The Walker Cricket Ground has been the home of Southgate Cricket Club since its foundation in 1855. The ground was originally called Chapel Fields and all club matches were staged here, including those involving United All England teams, the MCC and Southgate Cricket Club. These matches attracted crowds of up to 10,000. The most famous Middlesex cricketing family - the seven Walker brothers - played their cricket at Waterfall Road, Southgate and the ground was given the name 'The Walker Cricket Ground' by a deed of trust in December 1907; the document was signed by Mr R. D. Walker, the last surviving brother. The record attendance for the only first-class match at Southgate was around 10,000 for the game between Middlesex and Kent in 1859. This picture of the ground was taken in June 1910 during the Southgate CC versus the MCC match and shows play in progress beneath the nearby Christ Church. *Author's collection*

Left:

Middlesex CCC staged a Sunday League match versus Kent at Southgate in 1991, their first visit to the ground since 1859. They have yet to return, although in April 1994 an England Amateur XI is due to host the first match against the touring New Zealand team at the Walker Cricket Ground. This view shows the modern pavilion during the winter of 1993-94 when refurbishment and alterations were in progress. The ground is shared with the Southgate Hockey Club. *Author*

SOUTHGATE C.C. V. M.C.C. 18.6.10.

Above:
Aerial view of Lord's in 1948.
Aerofilms

Northamptonshire

NORTHAMPTONSHIRE

County Cricket Ground, Northampton.

Above:
Northamptonshire CCC moved to Wantage Road in 1886 from Northampton Racecourse. The ground is situated in the Abingdon district, east of the town centre, and was laid out under the guidance of H. H. Stephenson by the Northampton County Cricket and Recreation Grounds Company Limited in 1885 for £2,000. The initial first-class match was staged against neighbours Leicestershire in 1905. This illustration shows the ground in 1905, viewed from the Football Ground End and looking towards the Main Pavilion, old Ladies' Pavilion and scoreboard. *Author's collection*

Above:
The County Ground has struggled for recognition and praise in recent years despite minor improvements; although it is now owned by the club's trustees, no major redevelopment has taken place. This should change when the football club moves to a new stadium out of town. Northampton is the only county headquarters where the cricket ground shares the playing area with a professional football league club. This picture shows cricket being played at Northampton under the football floodlight pylons in 1993. *Author*

Top:
The club badge of Northamptonshire CCC. *County Print Services*

Above:

The County Ground is shared with
Football League Division Three side
Northampton Town Football Club -
association football has been played on
the ground since 1897 - which restricts
home fixtures at the beginning and end
of the cricket season. The Main
Pavilion was originally shared with the
football and bowling clubs but is now
solely used by the cricket club. The
whole playing area is 8.5 acres and is
used jointly by the football and cricket
clubs although the overlap between
pitches is little more than 20 metres.
The record attendance for a single
day's play was 21,770 versus the
touring Australians in 1953 with a total
of 31,000 attending the three days of
the match. This aerial photograph of
the ground was taken in 1951 and
shows a match in progress. *Aerofilms*

Above:

A new players' pavilion was built in
1979, with funds generated from an
appeal, to replace the old Ladies'
Pavilion. This houses executive boxes,
players' dressing rooms and the club
offices at first floor level. Further work
was carried out in 1987 and 1988 to
join the new pavilion to the Main
Stand and increase the size of the club
offices.

The old pavilion, named the
Spencer Pavilion in 1991, was
refurbished during the winter of
1990-91 and now includes a bar and
club room, a sponsors' area and
increased open and covered seating for
members' with coloured plastic tip-up
seats. This picture shows a view of play
in progress in 1993 *Author*

Below:
Founded in 1906, the Luton Town Cricket Club play at Wardown Park, a pleasant tree-enclosed ground to the north of the town centre. This picture shows an aerial view taken in 1929. *Aerofilms*

Right:
Since 1929 the ground has been levelled, creating raised banking on the east side of the ground by the Old Bedford Road, which provides an excellent position to view the cricket. This picture shows the ground in 1986 taken from the members' enclosure adjoining the pavilion. *Author*

LUTON

Above:
Wardown Park has been used by Northamptonshire CCC since 1973 for one-day matches with such success that in 1986 the county decided to stage a first-class match at Luton. The inaugural match against Yorkshire provided the record attendance for a first-class match of 3,500. Little has changed since 1929 other than the pavilion extension and the modern computerized scoreboard. This picture shows a view of the pavilion situated within the trees at the Park End. *Author*

Right:
The highest individual innings in a first-class match at Luton is 200 no by Robert Bailey for Northamptonshire versus Yorkshire in 1986.
County Print Services

Nottinghamshire

Trent Bridge.
Empics

Right:
The club badge of Nottinghamshire CCC.
County Print Services

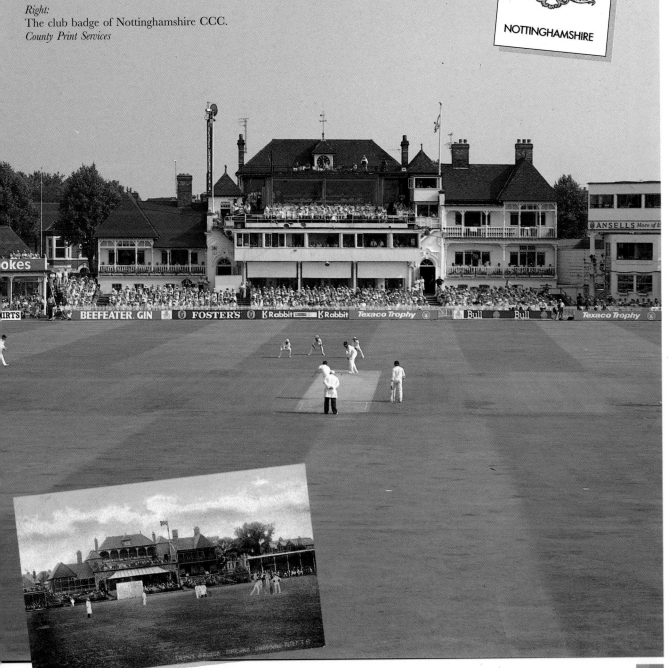

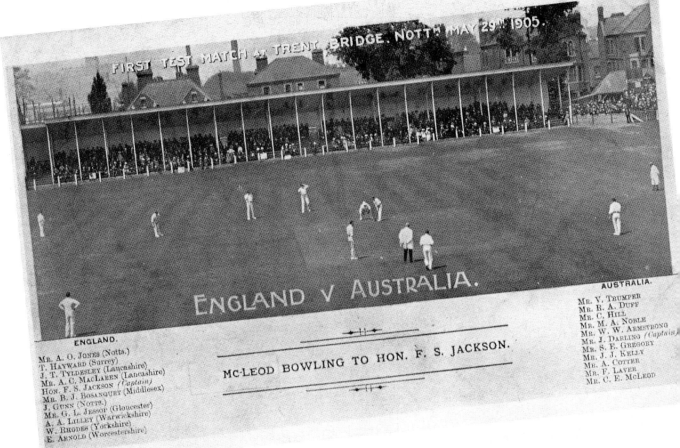

FIRST TEST MATCH AT TRENT BRIDGE. NOTT. MAY 29th 1905.

ENGLAND V AUSTRALIA.

ENGLAND.
Mr. A. O. Jones (Notts.)
T. Hayward (Surrey)
J. T. Tyldesley (Lancashire)
Mr. A. C. MacLaren (Lancashire)
Hon. F. S. Jackson (Captain)
Mr. B. J. Bosanquet (Middlesex)
J. Gunn (Notts.)
Mr. G. L. Jessop (Gloucester)
A. A. Lilley (Warwickshire)
W. Rhodes (Yorkshire)
E. Arnold (Worcestershire)

McLEOD BOWLING TO HON. F. S. JACKSON.

AUSTRALIA.
Mr. V. Trumper
Mr. R. A. Duff
Mr. C. Hill
Mr. M. A. Noble
Mr. W. W. Armstrong
Mr. J. Darling (Captain)
Mr. S. E. Gregory
Mr. J. J. Kelly
Mr. A. Cotter
Mr. F. Laver
Mr. C. E. McLeod

Right:
Trent Bridge became a cricket ground due to the enterprise of William Clarke and it was not until 1881 that the owners of the ground, the Chaworth-Musters family, signed a 99-year lease with Nottinghamshire CCC for both the Trent Bridge Inn and ground. This picture shows a china statue of William Clarke produced by the county club in 1988 as part of its 150th anniversary appeal. *Author*

Above:
In 1919 Nottinghamshire CCC purchased both the Inn, which they later sold, and the ground, which has been in their sole ownership since that date. This picture taken from the pavilion, looking down the wicket towards the Radcliffe Road End, shows play in progress during the first match of the England versus Australia Test Series of 1905 with McLeod bowling to Jackson. *Author's collection*

Previous page:
The present Members' Pavilion was built in 1886 and designed by architect Mr H. M. Townsend of Peterborough. It has since been altered and extended but much of its original character remains. This picture shows the pavilion in 1905 *Author*

Below:

Many developments have taken place at Trent Bridge over the years so that the ground, located close to the West Bridgford district of Nottingham, is now one of the best equipped Test Match venues in the country. This aerial picture shows the ground in 1952 before the construction of the new Nottinghamshire County Council offices, the new scoreboard and the redevelopment of the Fox Road side of the ground. It also shows clearly the location of Parr's Tree, which stood close to the Bridgford Road side of the ground behind the Parr Stand before it was blown down during a gale in January 1976. *Aerofilms*

Right:

Parr's Tree was an elm which gained its name in the last century from the frequency with which George Parr (1826-1891, Nottinghamshire CCC 1845-1870) managed to hit a cricket ball into its branches. Mini cricket bats have been made from the tree and this picture depicts one such bat. *Author*

Inset:
During the winter of 1978-79 new squash courts and the Nottinghamshire CCC general offices were built near the members' entrance at the Dixon Gates. Recently, in 1985, the Larwood and Voce Stand was added and behind it the Tavern public house, entered from the Fox Road side of the ground. During the winter of 1989-90 part of the Bridgford Road Stand was demolished and replaced by the William Clarke Stand, creating additional open seating for 2,000 and a new press box. This picture shows a view of the pavilion and the ground during the match between Nottinghamshire and the touring Pakistan team in 1987. *Author*

Above:
The Cyril Lowater Pavilion and Ladies' Pavilion were demolished during the winter of 1992-93 to make way for the New Stand, opened during the England versus Australia Test Match in 1993.

This picture shows the New Stand built by Wimpey Construction, with the 1993 Ashes Test Match in progress, viewed from the Radcliffe Road Stand. *Author*

Far right:
The highest individual innings in a first class match at Trent Bridge is 345 by Charlie Macartney for the touring Australians versus Nottinghamshire in 1921. *Author's collection*

C. G. MACARTNEY

Following pages:

This 1952 picture is an aerial view of the ground from the Radcliffe Road End looking towards the Main Pavilion, Lowater Pavilion and Ladies' Pavilion. It shows the size of the original grassed playing area. To the far right is the Trent Bridge Inn. The ground has been used for association football by both Nottingham Forest Football Club and Notts County Football Club, whose grounds are now within walking distance of Trent Bridge on either side of the nearby River Trent. The largest crowd to attend a single day's play at Trent Bridge was 35,000 for the Test Match between England and Australia in 1938 and for the Nottinghamshire versus Surrey County Championship match in 1948. Trent Bridge provides a good view of the play from every position and the most recent buildings - the William Clarke Stand and the Larwood and Voce Tavern Stand and the New Stand - all provide excellent seating and splendid facilities in keeping with the traditions of the ground.

Spectators still have direct access to the Trent Bridge Inn for refreshments. This picture shows a view of the pavilion taken in 1993.
Aerofilms

101

Above

The first cricket match staged at Worksop was in 1880 when Nottingham played against the Twenty-two of Sheffield, however, the initial first-class match staged by Nottinghamshire CCC at the present Central Avenue ground was in 1921 against Derbyshire. Central Avenue is the home of Worksop Town Cricket Club and much of the land for the ground was given to the club in 1900 by William Allen, a director of a local brewery, who also financed the building of the original pavilion, shown in this picture. The previous ground used by Worksop Town CC was situated in Bridge Street, where the main Bus Station is now located, south of the River Ryton which bounds the ground at the Central Avenue End. A valuable piece of land close to the town centre,

the present ground was used for agricultural purposes before it was levelled. Some locals said at the time that an error had been made as the pitch today lies four to five feet below the water level of the nearby Chesterfield Canal.

This aerial view shows Central Avenue from the pavilion, looking across the ground towards the Worksop Town FC football ground side and the town centre. The original pavilion was opened in 1901 before a match between Worksop Town CC and a Nottinghamshire Club and Ground XI but the match was abandoned without a ball being bowled due to heavy rain. The pavilion was demolished in 1972 and replaced by a new structure with squash courts as well as changing rooms for cricketers. During the winter of

1986-87 the cricket club decided to build its own pavilion. An extension was added to the existing structure which provides ample facilities, including a players' area in the front which over-looks the pitch. The pavilion and scoreboard are the only permanent buildings for cricket on the ground but on the football ground side are several stands and terraces belonging to the football club. The largest attendance for a match at Central Avenue was in 1966 when some 7,000 saw the Nottinghamshire versus Yorkshire County Championship match. *Aerofilms*

Inset:
Play in progress in 1986 viewed from the new pavilion enclosure. *Author*

Somerset

SOMERSET

Above:
The County Ground in St James's Street has been the headquarters of Somerset CCC since 1882. The county club acquired the ground from the Taunton Athletic Company and secured a lease for the ground in 1885. In 1882 the initial first-class match on the ground was staged against

Hampshire with the first County Championship match against Lancashire in 1891. The record attendance for a first-class match at Taunton was 10,000 in 1948 when the touring Australians visited the most westerly county ground on the circuit. This picture of the ground was taken in 1920 and shows a match in progress. *Author's collection*

Above:
Somerset CCC have shown great interest over the years in improving facilities at the County Ground, which is located close to the River Tone. A running track, later used for greyhound racing, was built around the perimeter of the cricket pitch at one time. The Old Pavilion, as it is known today, was erected with the Ridley Stand, which is situated under the shadow of St James's Church and the River Stand was built in 1955 from funds generated by the Somerset Supporters' Club. This picture shows an aerial view of the ground in 1952 with a match in progress. *Aerofilms*

Top:
The club badge of Somerset CCC. *County Print Services*

Above:

The County Ground is also used by Taunton Cricket Club and the Somerset Stragglers Cricket Club who have small separate pavilions opposite the new pavilion. The past decade has seen vast improvements at Taunton as a result of the achievements in limited-overs competitions. Much of the prize money has been spent on building a new pavilion and executive boxes and a scoreboard was presented by Saab UK in 1981. More recently, the Somerset Cricket Museum opened in 1989 in a small barn at the rear of the club shop on the Priory Bridge Road side of the ground. This redevelopment, together with a number of other small refurbished barns, has provided stores, offices, refreshment facilities and the Somerset Cricket Library, which is well worth a visit. This picture shows an aerial view of the ground in 1972 before much of the development took place. *Aerofilms*

Above right:

In 1990 the pavilion was named the Colin Atkinson Pavilion after the former well known and respected Somerset captain. It is often said by local cricket followers, 'If you can see the Quantock Hills it is going to rain and if you can't see them it is already raining'. However, the new pavilion has its back to the hills and the members can no longer see them! This 1993 picture shows the new pavilion. *Author*

Inset:

The best bowling performance in an innings in a first-class match at Taunton is 10 for 42 by Australian Albert Trott for Middlesex versus Somerset in 1900. *Author's collection*

Below left:
Somerset CCC's first match at Bath was in 1880 versus Sussex and their initial first-class match was against Hampshire in 1884. The Recreation Ground is situated almost in the middle of the Roman city; it lies at the bottom of the hollow in which Bath nestles, next to the River Avon and close to Bath Abbey. The Recreation Ground is shared with the Bath Rugby Football Club and is entered from William Street via Great Pultney Street through a fine turnstile. This picture of the ground was taken in 1908.
Author's collection

Below:
The players' pavilion is the only permanent feature on the ground - the rest of the temporary accommodation is only provided during festival weeks. The Recreation Ground is only used for cricket by Somerset CCC for a single week and should not be confused with Bath Cricket Club or Lansdown Cricket Club who play at another ground on the other side of North Parade Road. The ground is maintained by the City of Bath Leisure Services Department.

This aerial photograph shows the ground in 1935 laid out ready for the Bath cricket festival.

The ground is now somewhat overshadowed by the new sports centre to the south. Author

Although within sight of Bath Abbey and the buildings of the city centre this urban sports ground has lost some of its charm. Being a local authority ground the small cricket square is wedged between the hockey, football and rugby pitches, a part of each serving as the cricket outfield in summer. *Aerofilms*

Inset:
The best bowling performance recorded in a first-class match for Somerset at Bath is 16 for 83 by J. C. White versus Worcestershire in 1919. *Authors collection*

Bath, Recreation Ground.

J. C. WHITE

SOMERSET

BATH

Right:
Somerset CCC first visited Clarence
Park in 1914 when both their
opponents won: Yorkshire by 140 runs
and Essex by 10 wickets. The third
match, with Northamptonshire, was
cancelled due to the outbreak of World
War 1 and county cricket did not
return to Clarence Park until 1919.
Located very close to the coast of
Somerset's popular holiday resort,
Clarence Park was given to the town in
1882 as a gift from Rebecca Davies in
memory of her husband Henry. The
single-storey pavilion, which is painted
white and green, dates from 1882 and
is the only permanent building on the
ground, as shown in this 1986 picture.
Author

Above
Clarence Park is a public park owned
by Woodspring District Council; it is
only used by Somerset for festival
cricket weeks in August. The best
attendance for a first-class match was
6,000 against Hampshire in 1947. The
ground at Weston-Super-Mare provides
an atmosphere similar to that of a first-
class match in the early years of this
century. This aerial view was taken in
1923. *Aerofilms*

Right:
The best bowling performance recorded
in a first-class match at Weston-Super-
Mare is 16 for 88 by J. A. Newman for
Hampshire versus Somerset in 1927.
Author's collection

Surrey

Tooting Common and was laid in March 1845 by Mr M. Turtle of Clapham Road for £300. This picture was taken from the pavilion and shows the Vauxhall End of the ground in 1904. *Author's collection*

Above
This picture, taken during the Test Match between England and Australia at The Foster's Oval in 1993, shows a view of the ground taken from the first floor balcony of the new members' pavilion, constructed during the winter of 1992-93. Further development was undertaken to the top balcony during last winter, ready for the 1994 season. *Author*

Top:
The club badge of Surrey CCC. *County Print Services*

Above left:
A member of the Walworth Cricket Club, Mr William Baker, came to the assistance of the Surrey County Cricket Club when he suggested that Kennington Oval, a market garden and the property of the Duchy of Cornwall, might be used for cricket. The Duchy was willing to let it as a cricket ground and a lease of 31 years was granted at £120 per year plus a further £20 in taxes. At the time of its conversion to a cricket ground, Kennington Oval was mainly an open space surrounded by a small hedge and the ground takes its name from the surrounding streets rather than the shape of the playing area. The original turf came from

Above:

The first recorded match at Kennington Oval was played in May 1845 between Mr Fould's XI and Mr Houghton's XI and the first match involving Surrey was in August 1845 between the Gentlemen of Surrey and the Players of Surrey. Following the meeting of the Montpelier Club in August 1845 at the Horns Tavern, Kennington, more than a hundred members of different local cricket clubs in the county proposed the formation of a club to represent the county of Surrey. The resolution was carried amidst cheering and the formal inauguration took place at the Horns Tavern in October 1845. The first Surrey CCC home match was staged with neighbours Kent in 1846, the first County Championship fixture was against Sussex in 1873 and the first Test Match was in 1880 between England and Australia. This picture shows the ground in 1912 during the match between Surrey and the touring South Africans. *Author's collection*

Left:

The Nets and the West Stand was demolished after the 1988 season to make way for a new complex, including an indoor cricket centre. The majority of this work was paid for by funds raised by the 'Save the Oval Appeal' with assistance from Foster's brewery. The Kennington Oval is today known as The Foster's Oval. This picture shows an aerial view of the Kennington Oval in 1955 during the England versus South Africa Test Match. *Aerofilms*

Right:

The highest individual innings for England in a Test Match at The Oval is 364 by Len Hutton versus Australia in 1938. *Author's collection*

L. HUTTON

Above right:
The Kennington Oval was used for association football in the 19th century and was the venue for the FA Cup Final in 1872 and from 1874 to 1892. The pavilion was built in 1896 and was designed by the architect Mr A. T. Muirhead who was also responsible for the design of Old Trafford pavilion in Manchester. This picture shows a view of the pavilion with play in progress during the 1920 season. *Ron Harries*

Right:
The best bowling performance recorded in a first-class match at The Oval is 15 for 57 by W. P. Howell for the touring Australians versus Surrey in 1899. *Author's collection*

Far right:
In 1990 Surrey CCC renamed all the stands after famous players who have represented the county club: the Laker Stand (formerly the Taverners Stand), the Lock Stand (formerly the Mound Stand), the Jardine Stand (formerly the Vauxhall East Stand), the Fender Stand (formerly the Vauxhall Centre Stand), the Gover Stand (formerly the Vauxhall West Stand), the Surridge Enclosure (formerly the West Terrace) and the Bedser Stand (formerly the West Stand and Nets Stand). The Peter May Enclosure remains as previously named.

This picture shows a view of the ground in 1957 with play in progress. Crowds at The Foster's Oval are restricted to the present ground capacity of 17,500 but the largest attendance over three days for a match at the ground was 80,000 for the Surrey versus Yorkshire County Championship fixture in 1906, when many spectators were required to stand all day. *Author's collection*

828 KENNINGTON OVAL. — LL.

W. P. HOWELL
COPYRIGHT PHOTO
BOLLAND HANWELL W. & SOUTHALL.

OVAL CRICKET GROUND, LONDON.

includes facilities for players and officials with changing areas and indoor nets within the Ken Barrington Centre to the rear and in the basement. The upper levels include two storeys of executive boxes and a new press room and media centre on the top floor. The Ken Barrington Centre offers probably the best facilities in Surrey and South London for a number of sports, including martial arts, circuit training, five-a-side football, six-a-side hockey, badminton, volleyball, aerobics, netball, short tennis, table tennis, golf practice and yoga. This picture shows the new Bedser Stand in 1992. *Author*

Top:
The west side of the pavilion has made way for the Bedser Stand, incorporating the Ken Barrington Sports Centre in the basement; construction being carried out by Eve Construction PLC at a cost of about £3 million. The complex was completed in 1991 and was opened by the Queen in July 1991 during the National Westminster Bank Trophy quarter-final between Surrey and Essex. The West Stand development, since renamed the Bedser Stand, includes open seating for members plus several bars, restaurants and refreshment areas. The building

Following pages:
This 1949 aerial view of the ground clearly shows that it is located in an urban setting. Overshadowed by the gas holders and blocks of flats, it retains a fine view of the tower of the Palace of Westminster and central London from the upper part of the pavilion. *Aerofilms*

Above:

Surrey CCC made their first visit to Guildford for a first-class match in their 1938 County Championship match against Hampshire, with the first two days of the match attracting a total crowd of 10,000 spectators. The present Woodbridge Road Ground was given to the city by Sir Harry Waechter-Bart in 1911 for cricket, cycling, military parades and charitable purposes. The Guildford Cricket Club was established in 1862 and the club was disbanded between 1914 and 1922, though after 1918 the club's players played under the name of the Guildford Wanderers Cricket Club. This aerial picture of the ground was taken in 1935. *Aerofilms*

Above right:

Reputed to be one of the few level playing areas in the city the lush Woodbridge Road Ground covers eight acres and is green with trees around most of its surround. The busy Woodbridge Road runs along the east side of the tree-lined area and at the far end from the pavilion spectators can see

brief glimpses through the poplar and beech trees of the Thameslink trains linking Bedford, London and Guildford. The only permanent buildings on the ground are the two-storey cricket pavilion with some terraced seating on either side, the groundsman's stores and the scoreboard which was built along the lines of the famous Sydney Cricket Ground scoreboard in Australia.

In 1988 Guildford CC celebrated a jubilee of county cricket in the town. Important events staged at Guildford

have included a one-day match between the Club Cricket Conference and the touring South Africans in 194? and ten years later the Queen and the Duke of Edinburgh attended a match against Hampshire and met both team The best crowd for a single day of first class cricket at Woodbridge Road was 7,000 for the visit of Hampshire in 1938. This picture shows a view of the ground in 1991. *Author*

Sussex

SUSSEX

Above:
The Sussex County Cricket Club moved its headquarters from the Brunswick Ground to Eaton Road, Hove in 1872. The turf from the former was removed, transported and relaid at Eaton Road. The initial first-class match staged by Sussex was against Gloucestershire in June 1872. The members' pavilion was built in the 1880s and extended in 1921, with a major refurbishment and a further extension in 1933; the upper pavilion was reconstructed in 1961. This picture shows an aerial view of the ground in 1914. *Aerofilms*

Above:
The main scoreboard, which dates from the 1930s, was presented by the Harmsworth family. A new East Stand was built in 1988 and has taken the place of the 'Cowshed', which was demolished the previous year to the displeasure of many members. A squash club exists to the north-west of the playing area near the Cox Memorial Garden. The largest attendance was 14,500 for the game against the Australians in 1948. This 1993 picture shows the view from the players' enclosure looking towards the main scoreboard and east side of the ground. *Author*

Top:
The club badge of Sussex CCC. *County Print Services*

Above:
The Gilligan Stand, housing indoor
practice nets, was not constructed until
1971. Hove is an enjoyable county
ground with pleasant local
surroundings. This picture shows a view
of the main permanent buildings on the
ground in 1920. *Author's collection*

Left:
Entry to the ground from Eaton Road
is through the Tate Memorial Gates. A
plaque marking the centenary of cricket
at Hove in 1972 can be found close to
the entrance. This aerial view of the
ground in 1950 with play in progress
shows the development which has taken
place since 1920. *Author's collection*

Bottom left:
The highest individual innings against
Sussex in a first-class match at Hove is
322 by E. Paynter for Lancashire in
1937. *County Print Services*

CHURCHMAN'S CIGARETTES

K. S. DULEEPSINHJI

Above:
An aerial view of the ground in 1972 during construction of the adjoining flats at the Sea End of the ground. *Aerofilms*

Right:
The highest individual innings for Sussex in a first-class match at Hove is 333 by K. S. Duleepsinhji versus Northamptonshire in 1930. *Author's collection*

Below:

The present ground and pavilion, situated to the north of Arundel Castle, was laid out by the 15th Duke of Norfolk in 1894-95. A superb setting for cricket, the work was continued by Bernard, the 16th Duke of Norfolk, one time MCC president. In 1975 Lavinia, Duchess of Norfolk decided that, as a memorial to her late husband, she should continue to stage cricket at Castle Park with the object of sustaining its unique character and to aid 'the promotion encouragement and maintenance of the playing of cricket'.

With some assistance she set about the task which led to the establishment of the Friends of Arundel Castle Cricket Club. The annual match with the touring team started in 1977 against the Australians when a crowd of some 6,000 attended. This aerial picture shows the ground in 1972. *Aerofilms*

Right:

The highest individual innings for Sussex in a first-class match at Arundel is 107 by Colin Wells versus Hampshire in 1990. *Sussex CCC*

ARUNDEL

Above:
In 1987 the Friends of Arundel Castle Cricket Foundation was established, assisted by a generous donation from Mr J. Paul Getty Jr, with the aim of providing cricket coaching for youngsters. The old Etonian and captain of Sussex CCC, John Barclay, was appointed director of cricket and coaching and in 1989 a new indoor cricket school was opened at the rear of the present pavilion (the pavilion was built 22yds long, the length of a cricket pitch). The ground slopes naturally from north-west to south-east but the cricket area has been levelled and is roughly circular. The entire area is enclosed by mature landscaped trees which provide a green backcloth to all activities on the field. Sussex CCC played their initial first-class County Championship match against Hampshire at Arundel in 1991. This 1992 picture shows a view of the pavilion surrounded by trees. *Author*

Above right:
Regrettably the hurricane in October 1987 removed many of the trees to the south and south-east but this has given a better view of the cathedral and castle from the bank at the Park End of the ground. This picture shows this view taken in 1993 during the match against the touring Australians when a record crowd of 15,000 was present. *Author*

S 10603   SAFFR

"THE SAFFRONS"

Right:

The home of Eastbourne Cricket Club, established in 1855, shares its outfield with Eastbourne Town Football Club. The sports complex is known today as the Eastbourne Saffrons Sports Club and it celebrated its centenary in 1986. The Saffrons Ground was laid out in 1884 but Sussex CCC did not play on the ground until 1897 when Middlesex visited. The name originates from the use to which the land was put over a century ago, when saffron was grown for dyeing and medicinal purposes. The part of the ground known as Larkin's Field dates from the 1700s when a saddler named Larkin rented the ground to graze the cattle he was raising for their hides. The Main Pavilion, built in 1884, was destroyed by fire in 1947. On the Old White Pavilion, which is known as the War Memorial Pavilion, and the squash courts, is a plaque bearing the name of the illustrious cricketer Douglas R. Jardine. The other pavilion on the ground is the Harry Bartlett Pavilion. This picture shows a view of the ground in 1929 with play in progress. *Author's collection*

Top:

This picture shows a view of the new pavilion built in 1947 which replaced the fire damaged existing building; it was itself damaged by fire in 1977.

Eastbourne was the ground where Archie MacLaren's Young Amateurs defeated the formidable Australians in 1921 - possibly the most famous match to have taken place on the ground. The record attendance for a first-class match was 5,000 for the visit of Somerset in 1948. *Author's collection*

122

Below:
From the pavilion a splendid view can be seen of Eastbourne Town Hall, with its fine clock tower and dome. This picture shows this view taken in 1988. *Author*

Far right:
The highest individual innings in a first-class match at Eastbourne is 310 by Harold Gimblett for Somerset versus Sussex in 1948. *County Print Services*

Right:
The best bowling performance in a first-class match at Eastbourne is 16 for 106 by R. C. Robert-Glasgow for Somerset versus Sussex in 1923. *Author's collection*

R. C. ROBERTSON GLASGOW

133-C   SOMERSET

H. GIMBLETT

RANJI, AND RELF BATTING ON HORSHAM
CRICKET GROUND JUNE 15./08 SUSSEX V. ESSEX.

Above:
The home of Horsham Cricket Club, established in 1771, the Cricket Field Road Ground has been in use since 1851. Sussex CCC played their initial first-class match against Essex at Horsham in 1908. This picture shows the match in progress with Ranjitsinhji and Relf batting for the home side.

The first pavilion (now demolished) was situated close to the footbridge crossing the railway line. The present pavilion was built in 1921.
Author's collection

Right:
The north side of the ground is bounded by the River Arun, close to where willow trees were planted by Ben Warsop, the former cricket bat manufacturer. A cricket ball has been hit into the river once, by Jacko Watson, the mightiest of Sussex hitters. The pleasing sound of bells ringing from the local St Mary's Church a short walk from the ground can he heard while watching a day's play. The best attendance for a first-class match was 6,000 against Northamptonshire in

1948. This picture shows a view of the pavilion and playing area in 1987.
Author

Right:
The best bowling performance recorded in a first-class match at Horsham is 15 for 173 by D. V. P. Wright for Kent versus Sussex in 1947.
County Print Services

124

Warwickshire

Right:
The club badge of Warwickshire CCC.
County Print Services

WARWICKSHIRE

SOUTH AFRICAN CRICKET TEAM, 1924.

R. H. CATTERALL   P. A. HANDS   E. P. NUPEN
H. W. TAYLOR (CAPTAIN)   J. M. BLANCKENBURG

D. J. MAINTJES   H. G. DEANE
C. P. CARTER   M. COMMAILLE

S. P. KINNEIR,
WARWICKSHIRE.

Opposite:

Edgbaston is the third ground in Birmingham to be used by Warwickshire CCC. The initial first-class match staged at Edgbaston was against Kent in 1894, although the first match was in 1886 between an England XI and the touring Australians. The ground was recognized as suitable for staging Test Matches when England met Australia in the first test of the 1902 series. The main part of the ground was acquired freehold by the reorganized Warwickshire CCC in 1886 and since then it has been added to piecemeal so that it is now one of the best-equipped cricket grounds in the country. This aerial view of the ground was taken in 1950 and shows that the only permanent buildings at that time were the pavilion and adjoining stands together with the Thwaite Scoreboard and old Priory Stand. The Hill Bank is little changed as is the Rea Bank Stand, although a roof has now been added.
Aerofilms

Previous page:

For the start of the 1989 season, as part of the ground development scheme, some key Warwickshire names were honoured: the executive club was renamed the Cyril Goodway Suite; the members' bar/lounge became the Tom Dollery Lounge; the Rea Bank Stand, the Eric Hollies Stand; the West Wing Stand, the R. V. Ryder Stand and the East Wing Stand, the Leslie Deakins Stand - the latter acknowledging the service to the county club of two secretaries during the years 1889 to 1976. Since 1989 the Aylesford Executive Boxes A to T situated above the Priory and Raglan Stands have been constructed and the county club propose to build additional executive boxes to the rear of the Hill Bank. Edgbaston is now more of a stadium with raised tiers of plastic seating on all sides; nevertheless, a backcloth of trees is still visible in many areas. This picture shows a view of the ground from the Ryder Stand taken in 1993 during the England versus Australia one-day international match. The record crowd at Edgbaston was 28,000 for the Warwickshire versus Lancashire County Championship match in 1951 and the record for a single day of a Test Match is 32,000 for the first day of the England-West Indies Test Match of 1957. *Author*

Above:
The lowest innings total against England in a Test Match at Edgbaston is 30 by South Africa in 1924.
Ron Harries

Above right:
The highest individual innings for Warwickshire in a first-class match at Edgbaston is 268 no by S. P. Kinneir versus Hampshire in 1911.
Author's collection

Previous pages:
The ground was formerly a 'meadow of rough grazing land' and belonged to Lord Calthorpe until he allowed Warwickshire CCC to lease it for cricket. The original pavilion remains but so much alteration has taken place that, except for part of the distinctive, red-tiled roof and weather vane, it is difficult to recognize it among all the additions at the Pavilion End. This picture shows an aerial view of the ground in 1958; included in this view is the pavilion, the Ryder Stand and the newly constructed Raglan and Priory Stands. *Aerofilms*

Above right:
A painting (by an unknown artist) of the pavilion area at Edgbaston in 1894, the year when Warwickshire achieved first-class status. *Ken Kelly*

Right:
A rural scene at Edgbaston during the 1887 match between Warwickshire and Derbyshire. George Davidson is bowling for Derbyshire to William Herbert Bainbridge, the Warwickshire captain, with William Storer as the Wicketkeeper. *Ken Kelly*

Below:
Edgbaston during the 1924 Test match against South Africa. Frank Wooley is batting. The scene is no longer rural as houses have been built in Constance Road, behind the scoreboard. *Ken Kelly*

Above:
Since the early 1960s much development has taken place at Edgbaston, including the William Ansell Stand which was built during the late 1950s from funds raised by the Warwickshire County Cricket Supporters' Association. The stand was named after a key figure in the early history of Edgbaston and Warwickshire CCC. In 1975 an executive suite was added to the William Ansell Stand and in recent seasons more sponsors' suites and plastic tip-up seats have been installed to improve the facilities for members. The majority of building took place in 1946 and thereafter various additions were made in the late 1950s and early 1960s. The Thwaite Memorial Scoreboard, built in 1950, was moved and reconstructed during the winter of 1988-89 during the improvements made to the Stanley Barnes Stand and to the seating at the City End of the ground (including an enlarged and improved area for disabled spectators). This aerial view of the ground was taken in 1972. Edgbaston is a welcoming ground to enter with its fine facilities, covered accommodation and permanent seating Lord's is its only superior in the country. *Aerofilms*

Left:
On the Edgbaston Road frontage spectators can see the Sydney Barnes Wicket Gate which is shown in this picture. The Warwickshire Indoor Cricket School, built in 1955, is located close to the members' entrance on Edgbaston Road. The most interesting innovation at Edgbaston in recent years has been the installation of a large mechanically operated pitch cover known as the 'Brumbreller'. *Author*

THE
SYDNEY BARNES
WICKET GATE

THIS GATE WAS ERECTED IN MEMORY OF
SYDNEY F. BARNES
(WARWICKSHIRE, LANCASHIRE,
STAFFORDSHIRE AND ENGLAND)
AND IS SITED APPROXIMATELY AT THE POINT
WHERE HE ENTERED THE EDGBASTON GROUND
ON THE 20TH. AUGUST, 1894
TO PLAY IN HIS FIRST COUNTY MATCH.
UNIVERSALLY ACKNOWLEDGED IN LATER YEARS
AS "THE GREATEST BOWLER OF THEM ALL". IT
SEEMED APPROPRIATE TO THE COMMITTEE OF
THE WARWICKSHIRE COUNTY CRICKET CLUB
TO PERPETUATE HIS MEMORY AT THIS POINT
WHERE HIS COUNTY CAREER COMMENCED
AND HIS ASHES NOW REST
1873 TO 1967

EDGBASTON   1973

Worcestershire

Worcester Cathedral & County Cricket Ground.

Left:
Probably the most attractive county ground in the country, it was the property of Worcester cathedral until purchased by the club in 1976 for £30,000. The view of the playing area from the pavilion enclosure has as its backcloth the 14th-century cathedral. This picture shows a view of the ground and cathedral taken from the pavilion in 1908. *Author's collection*

Above:
This picture shows an aerial view of the ground in 1974. *Aerofilms*

Top:
The club badge of Worcestershire CCC. County Print Services

Right main picture:
The County Cricket Ground at Worcester is situated in New Road, west of the bridge crossing the River Severn and within walking distance of the city centre. This aerial picture shows the ground in 1920. *Aerofilms*

Below:
Worcestershire CCC moved to New Road in 1899 from Boughton Park and the initial first-class match staged was against Yorkshire in May 1899. The members' pavilion was built in 1898-99 and remains little changed today externally, although internal alterations have taken place. This picture shows the pavilion in 1905. *Author's collection*

Inset far right:
Regular floods from the nearby River Severn have on occasions introduced fishing, boating, swimming and even ice skating to the County Ground! In the members' pavilion there is a brass plate showing the highest water level in 1947 - some 3.5ft above the floor and several feet above the playing area outside. The flooding usually occurs around Christmas but as recently as 1987 flooding took place in March, only a few weeks before the start of the season.

Since 1951, when Worcestershire CCC Supporters' Association was established, significant improvements have taken place at the County Ground. These have included the addition of new seating in 1952 on the western side of the ground, a scoreboard in 1954 and two years later

the Ladies' Pavilion. In 1965 the Severn Bar on the east side was rebuilt and in the winter of 1973-74 major additions were made to the New Road Stand, notably a roof, press box/scorers room and the secretary's office. The largest crowd was 14,000 for a match against the Australians in 1948.

During the winter of 1984-85 further development was undertaken when an executive suite was built on the site of the old supporters' association offices, scorers' room and press box. The scorers' room and press box were moved to the other end of the New Road Stand, near to the pavilion. The Worcestershire CCC Supporters' Association is now housed in the offices of the club's marketing department and adjoining this an indoor sports complex and cricket nets are scheduled to be built. The winter of 1989-90 saw the construction of new executive boxes on top of the New Road Stand and since then almost all the seating within the ground has been changed to the plastic tip-up variety in the club colours of green and white. This picture shows the pavilion in 1993. *Author*

Right inset:
The best bowling performance recorded in a first-class match at Worcester is 15 for 106 by R. D. Perks for Worcestershire versus Essex in 1937. *Author's collection*

THE PAVILION—WORCESTERSHIRE COUNTY CRICKET GROUND.

Photo by Bennett & Sons, Worcester.

Above and right:

The Kidderminster Cricket Club was established in 1890 and its ground, located close to the main Chester Road, was originally part of the land near Offmore Farm belonging to the Earl of Dudley's estate. The ground was opened in August 1870 and by 1896 the club had secured the lease direct from the Earl of Dudley; this was renewed annually until 1918 when the Dudley property was sold at auction. Mr Michael Tomkinson, a local carpet manufacturer, the then President of the club, purchased the freehold for £1,287 10s in December 1918 with a view to taking over when finances permitted. The original Old Pavilion was brought by the club from their previous Worcester Road ground and rebuilt on its present site in 1896. The new pavilion was built in 1925 at a cost of £886 raised by the members to commemorate winning the Birmingham League in 1924. The first Worcestershire CCC match staged at Kidderminster was for the 1921 visit of Glamorgan. After 46 consecutive seasons the run ended - possibly because Worcestershire were bowled out for 63 in one match - but in 1987 first-class cricket returned to Kidderminster and since then a single County Championship match has been staged each season. The largest attendance was 7,000 for a match against Yorkshire in 1956. These pictures show views of the old and new pavilions in 1994. *Author*

Right:

The highest individual innings in a first-class match at Kidderminster is 259 by Don Kenyon for Worcestershire versus Yorkshire in 1956. *Author's collection*

Yorkshire

YORKSHIRE

A ground view of Headingley during the 1992 Benson & Hedges Cup match between Yorkshire and Nottinghamshire.

Above:
The club badge of Yorkshire CCC.
County Print Services

Above:

The city of Leeds can thank a group of wealthy gentlemen developers who were also sportsmen who joined together to buy lot 17a - a plot of land to the north-west of Leeds - at an auction by the Cardigan Estate. They formed the Leeds Cricket, Football and Athletic Company Limited and their chairman was Lord Hawke, who himself captained Yorkshire CCC from 1883 to 1910. The purchase was the first major step towards the establishment of the county's cricket headquarters at Headingley.

Cricket and rugby football have been played at Headingley since 1890 when the first important cricket match was staged between the North and the touring Australians. The next year saw Yorkshire's initial first-class match on the ground against Kent and in 1899 Headingley staged its first Test Match between England and Australia. Yorkshire CCC moved its headquarters to Leeds in 1903 - it had previously leased offices in Park Road, Leeds - and today leases its administrative offices, built in 1962 in the north-east corner of the ground, from the Leeds Cricket, Football and Athletic Company Limited at Headingley. This aerial picture of the ground was taken in 1923 and shows the members' pavilion and Main Football Stand viewed from the Kirkstall Lane End of the ground.
Aerofilms

Left:
The highest individual innings in a first-class match at Headingley is 334 by Don Bradman for Australia versus England during the 1930 Test Match.
Author's collection

considerable amount of the ...velopment at Headingley was ...ndertaken by Sir Edwin Airey, a local ...ilding contractor, who in 1932 ...rted improvements designed to ...tablish Headingley as a major ...icketing venue in England. The dual-...urpose Football or Main Stand ...etches along the southern boundary ...the outfield and from it one can view ...icket to the north or rugby league ...otball to the south (Headingley is also ...e home of the Leeds Rugby League ...ootball Club). The Leeds Pavilion is ...e oldest building on the ground and ...uses the Leeds Company office and ...embers' dining rooms, function suites, ...veral bars and a restaurant. There are ...so a number of hospitality rooms, ...staurants and bars for use by ...onsors. Other additions include the ...irkstall Lane End and the Winter ...hed Stand, containing executive boxes ...nd ample seating. Since 1989 all ...ating in the ground, including the vast ...est Terrace and North Enclosure ...eas, is of the plastic tip-up variety. In

1981 the computerised scoreboard was installed, sponsored by the Scottish and Newcastle Brewery. The Sutcliffe Gates in St Michael's Lane form the main entrance to the ground and just opposite is the new Yorkshire CCC Indoor Cricket School and library. This aerial picture of the ground was taken in 1968 and shows the new stands built since 1932. *Aerofilms*

Below right:

A £2.5 million refurbishment programme to improve facilities at Headingley was announced in 1989 and work started soon afterwards. A large executive and hospitality complex is planned for the top level of the restructured Main Stand and additional new seating is awaited. 1991 saw the opening of the Jim Kilburn Press Gallery located on the ground floor of the Main Stand behind the bowler's arm at the Football Stand End. The new press box was

opened on the morning of the Test Match between England and the West Indies by former Yorkshire Post cricket writer Jim Kilburn. The ground was renamed Bass Headingley in 1990 after the brewery had provided money for the ground improvements. During the winter of 1992-93 the Leeds Pavilion received a major facelift; the refurbishment to the interior and exterior has returned the structure to its original splendour, as seen in the 1923 view (page 138) and the changing rooms and viewing area have been moved beneath the Main Football Stand.

This picture shows the ground from the Western Terrace during the 1993 Test Match between England and Australia. *Author*

Yorkshire CCC played their initial first-class match at Horton Park Avenue, known today as Bradford Park Avenue, in June 1881 versus Kent. To many supporters Bradford Park Avenue was the ideal Yorkshire CCC home venue with its splendid Victorian pavilion and ample benched seating on raised concrete whitewashed terracing. The ground previously adjoined the football ground of Bradford Park Avenue Football Club and this is shown in the aerial picture from 1934. *Aerofilms*

Opposite:

This aerial view shows Bradford Park Avenue as it was in 1972 before much of the demolition which took place

during the 1980s when Yorkshire CCC ceased to use the ground. In light of the Taylor Report, following the fire at Bradford City's football ground at Valley Parade, major improvements were required to the ground and its facilities and cricket left Bradford Park Avenue in 1985 and did not return for a County Championship match until 1992. *Aerofilms*

Below right:

The best bowling performance recorded for Yorkshire in a first-class match at Bradford is 14 for 68 by H. Verity versus Glamorgan in 1939.
County Print Services

Inset top:

Inset left:

Constructed at the former Football Ground End in a large industrial unit/warehouse is the privately owned Speedball Indoor Cricket Centre. The pavilion, Football Stand and most of the out-buildings were finally demolished during the winter of 1987-88. The only permanent structures which remain are the concrete terraces, the scoreboard and the groundsman's stores. Any cricket spectator who remembers Bradford Park Avenue as it was 10-15 years ago will be surprised to see the ground today as it has lost all of its charm.

The Park Avenue ground is now owned by Bradford Metropolitan Council and they have offered considerable support to the Friends of Bradford Park Avenue Cricket Society with a 999 year lease at a nominal rent, £15,000 per annum for five years towards the up-keep of the grounds and £40,000 towards ground improvements. A further £60,000 has been obtained from sponsorship, donations and other fund-raising activities and Yorkshire CCC have set up an Academy for Young Cricketers at the ground. During the winter of 1990-91 new changing rooms and refreshment facilities were constructed and six new pitches were laid. A further six pitches were laid during the next winter and improvements to spectator and player facilities followed during the winter months of 1992-93 and 1993-94. This 1991 picture shows a view of the ground from the former Pavilion End looking towards the old Football Ground End and the city of Bradford beyond. The largest crowd to attend a first-class match at Bradford Park Avenue was 30,790 for the Yorkshire versus Gloucestershire County Championship match in 1947. *Author*

Inset left:
The highest individual innings in a first-class match against Yorkshire at Bradford is 234 by C. B. Fry for Sussex in 1903. *Author's collection*

HARROGATE

Leicestershire. The main pavilion for players and members was built in 1896, the Mound Stand was constructed in 1956 and the Tavern Bar and Restaurant was built in 1965. The ground was for many years owned by the town cricket club but in 1936, during a difficult period in the club's history, the ground was purchased by the Harrogate Corporation, who still own it. This aerial picture of the ground was taken in 1972 and shows the main pavilion, Mound Stand and scoreboard. *Aerofilms*

Top:
The pride and joy of Harrogate's cricket supporters was Maurice Leyland, undoubtedly the finest local player ever produced, who represented his home town club Harrogate Cricket Club, Yorkshire CCC and England. Appropriately, the Leyland Gates welcome you at one of the ground's entrances, approached from St Mark's

Avenue. The gates were erected in 1965, two years before Leyland's death. The Centenary Gates, erected in 1977, form the main entrance to the ground from St George's Road. This picture shows the pavilion and adjoining Tavern in 1988. The best crowd for a single day's play at St George's Road was 15,000 when India played Pakistan for the charity Help the Aged in 1986. However, the best attendance for a Yorkshire CCC match was 13,630 for the County Championship match with Glamorgan in 1962. Author

Above left:
On 14 June 1991 a visit to St George's Road Cricket Ground was made by HRH The Duchess of Kent - Patroness of Yorkshire CCC for 25 years - when the County Championship match in progress was with Kent. This picture shows the First Day Cover which was issued by Stamp Publicity to celebrate this visit. *Author's collection*

Left:
The best bowling performance recorded in a first-class match at Harrogate is 14 for 64 by Ray Illingworth for Yorkshire versus Gloucestershire in 1967.
County Print Services

Opposite:
The St George's Road Ground has been the home of Harrogate Cricket Club since its establishment in 1877. The initial first-class match staged at Harrogate was in 1882 when an England XI played the touring Australians (this match was also the first in England to commence on a Saturday) and the first County Championship match at Harrogate was in 1894 when Yorkshire played

Above:
Situated in the pleasant suburb of
Acklam on the southern outskirts of
Middlesbrough, Acklam Park in Green
Lane has been since 1932 the home
ground of Middlesbrough Cricket Club,
established in 1875. The 12-acre
ground includes not only the main
cricket ground but also two full size
rugby football pitches. The whole
ground is in excellent condition and the
pavilion, which is at right-angles to the
wicket, includes changing rooms and a
large dining room over-looking the
playing area. To the rear of the pavilion is the Middlesbrough CC clubhouse
which has two attractively furnished
bars. The scoreboard has been mod-
ernised and is now fully automatic; it
has been built on two levels, the lower
being a store for the groundsman's
equipment and the upper level the
scorebox. This aerial picture of

the ground was taken in
1964. *Aerofilms*

Right
The initial first-class
County Championship
match staged by
Yorkshire at Acklam
Park was in 1956
against Glamorgan
when 9,423 spectators
attended the first two days of the
match, the third day being abandoned
due to poor weather. The main pavilion and most of the banking surrounding the playing area were built in 1953
thanks to Mr J. Eric Thomas, the chairman, and Mr H. E. Thomas, the club
secretary. This picture shows the
ground in 1988 during the County
Championship match between
Yorkshire and Hampshire. The best

crowd to attend a match at
Middlesbrough was 13,100 for the visit
of Warwickshire in 1967. *Author*

Inset:
The highest individual innings in a first
class match at Middlesbrough is 253 no
by Alan Wells for Sussex versus
Yorkshire in 1991. *Sussex CCC*

Right:
The North Marine Road cricket ground was leased by Scarborough Cricket Club from 1863 for £15 a year until it was purchased in 1878. The first Scarborough cricket festival was staged in 1876 and the first first-class match staged by Yorkshire CCC at North Marine Road was versus I'Zingari in 1878. This picture of the ground was taken in 1905 and shows Wilfred Rhodes bowling to Warwick Armstrong. *Author's collection*

Below:
This picture shows a view of the pavilion in 1991, little changed from the 1905 view. The largest attendance for a first-class match at Scarborough was 22,946 for the County Championship match between Yorkshire and Derbyshire in 1947. *Author*

SCARBOROUGH

The original pavilion erected in 1874 was replaced at a cost of £2,150 in 1895 by a new pavilion which still stands in the north-west corner of the ground. Before the first County Championship match on the ground, staged by Yorkshire against Leicestershire in 1896, the pavilion clock was presented as a gift to the club by Mr and Mrs J. Compton-Rickett and Mr J. H. Morton.

In 1902, thanks to funds generated from a successful festival, a new seating enclosure was erected; it was added to in the following year and in 1907. In 1903 a press box/scorers' room was constructed at a cost of £250 but it was not until after World War 1 that further development took place when a concrete stand was built in the north-east corner of the ground in 1926. This picture shows a view of the pavilion with play in progress during the festival of 1953. *Author's collection*

Opposite
The West Stand built in 1956 is the most recent addition to the ground; it is shown clearly to the right of the playing area in this aerial picture. *Aerofilms*

Below:
A view of the ground and pavilion during the Scarborough festival week in 1988. The annual Scarborough festival matches are among the most successful involving county teams. *Author*

CRICKET GROUND, SCARBOROUGH

L 5143

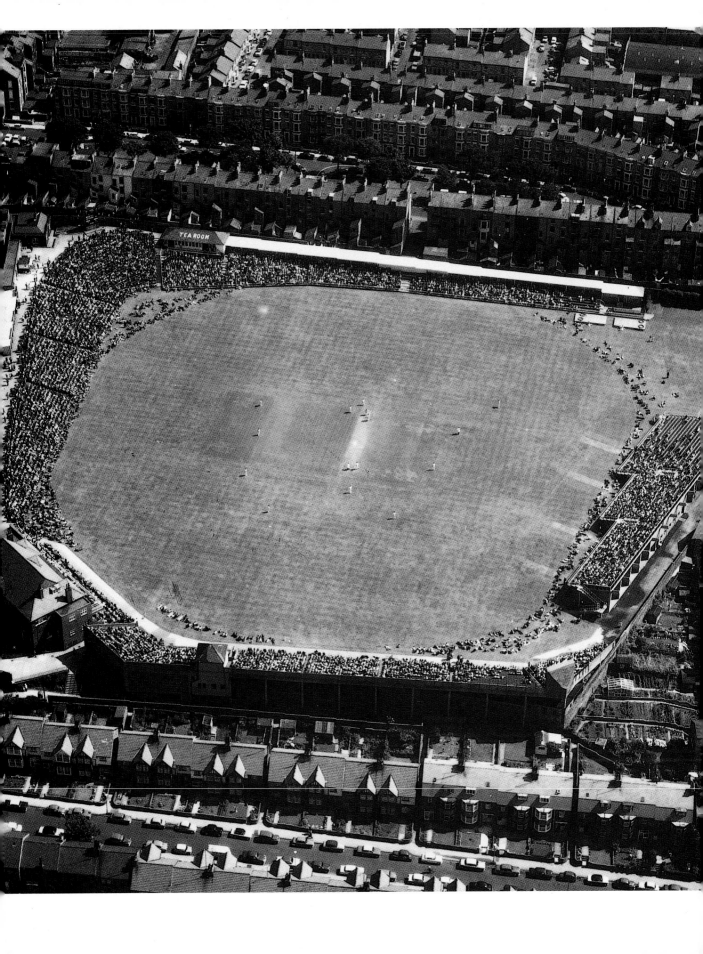

Above:

From 1855 to 1973 cricket in Sheffield, including a single Test Match between England and Australia in 1902, was staged at Bramall Lane on the ground shared with Sheffield United Football Club. The continued encroachment of association football finally put an end to first-class cricket at Bramall Lane and the last County Championship match was with Lancashire. The historic turf was sold to Sheffield cricket-lovers, whilst bulldozers moved in within a week to prepare for the construction of a new football stand for Sheffield United. Yorkshire CCC finally made a commitment to stage first-class cricket in Sheffield at Abbeydale Park and their initial first-class match was in May 1974 versus Warwickshire. This picture shows an aerial view of the ground at Bramall Lane in 1972. *Aerofilms*

Right:

In 1973 the Sheffield Cricket-lovers Society produced a commemorative china plate to mark the last first-class match at Bramall Lane - the Roses encounter with Lancashire. Shown in his picture it was issued by a well known local cricket-lover and Yorkshire CCC committee member, Mr David Drabble of Dronfield. *Author*

Inset:

Abbeydale Park is located on the south-western outskirts of Sheffield in a small village called Dore on the Yorkshire-Derbyshire border - closer to the Peak District National Park than to the Yorkshire Dales. Until county boundary changes, the ground was in Derbyshire and was used by Derbyshire CCC from 1946 to 1947. The Abbeydale Park ground is the home both of Sheffield Collegiate Cricket Club, which was established in 1881, and the Sheffield Amateur Sports Club (SASC), which hosts many sports. Several improvements have been made since the first county match in 1974, but naturally it has not been SASC's aim to convert Abbeydale into another Bramall Lane. SASC believes it has one of the premier sports grounds of its kind in the country and the success achieved so far suggests this is the kind of venue that spectators enjoy watching cricket being played at; this picture shows a view of the fine pavilion with its excellent facilities in 1991.

The ground is located on a slope although the square is flat. During the winter of 1991-92 much of the playing area was re-levelled so that the slope towards the hockey ground is now not so severe. Abbeydale Park is one of the more attractive out grounds; in its open, idyllic setting it is a contrast to the traditional stadium-like grounds used by Yorkshire. The best attendance for a first-class match at Abbeydale Park was 8,000 for the match with the touring West Indians in 1976. *Author*

Oxford

aerial view of 1932 shows the ground within the University Parks. *Aerofilms*

Inset:
The highest individual innings for Oxford University in a first-class match at the University Parks is 236 by E. R. T. Holmes versus the Free Foresters in 1927. *Author's collection*

Below left:
The University Parks cover about 65 acres and are open to the public. The first match was played in 1881 by which time the pavilion had been built to the designs of Sir Thomas G. Jackson, architect of many 19th-and early 20th-century buildings in Oxford. This 1991 picture shows a view of the pavilion which is the main focus of the ground. It is an impressive building with three striking gables in its steeply pitched roof, surmounted by a cupola. Part of the verandah has been enclosed to provide a press box. The Long Room, with its large roof trusses, is reminiscent of a university hall; the walls are in panelled oak, on which the names of all Blues are recorded in gold lettering. *Author*

Top:
The first mention of cricket in Oxford appears to have been in 1727 but the Oxford University Cricket Club did not play in a match until 1827. Initial matches were played at Cowley Marsh until in 1881 Dr Evans, Master of

Pembroke College, succeeded in obtaining a lease on 10 acres of land in the University Parks. This venue remains the club's home ground and many consider it to be one of the most attractive venues in the country. This

Top right:
This picture shows the famous club colours of Oxford University CC with an inset of C. B. Fry who represented the side between 1892 and 1895. County Print Services

Cambridge

MR S.M.J. WOODS
*Cambridge University/
Somerset*

Opposite:
Founded in 1820 the Cambridge University Cricket Club has played all its home matches at Fenner's University Cricket Ground in the centre of the city since 1848. The ground, which is sited to the east of Parkers' Piece, was leased from Gonville and Caius College in 1846 by Mr F. P. Fenner. This picture shows an aerial view of the ground in 1928. The freehold of the University Cricket Ground was acquired from the college in 1894 and assigned to a company which held it in trust until in 1976 the University assumed full financial responsibility for the ground. *Aerofilms*

Above:
Fenner's was shared until 1950 with the University Athletics Club; surrounding the playing area was a running track,

which has now been removed. The old pavilion was sited on the south-west side backing onto Gresham Road, but in 1972 a new pavilion was designed by architect Sir Colin Stansfield-Smith RIBA (Cricket Blue 1954-57) and was built on the Wollaston Road side on the north-east. This picture shows the new pavilion which provides much better accommodation, although some spectators still prefer the character of the former pavilion. *Author*

Right inset:
The highest first-class innings total at Fenner's Cricket Ground of 730 for 3 declared was recorded by the West Indies versus Cambridge University in 1950. *Author's collection*

Above inset:
The best bowling performance recorde for Cambridge University in a first-clas match at Fenner's Cricket Ground is 1 for 88 by S. M. J. Woods versus C. I. Thornton's XI in 1890.
County Print Services

Top:
This picture shows the club colours of Cambridge University CC with an inse of Mike Brearley who captained the side in 1963 and 1964.
County Print Service

WEST INDIES CRICKET TEAM.

Back row - Left to right:-
A. Ganteaume, N. Asgarali, F. Alexander, D. Atkinson, T. Dewdney, W. Hall, G. Sobres, B. Pairaudeau,
R. Gilchrist, C. Smith.
Front row - Left to right:-
S. Ramadhin, F. M. Worrell, J. D. Goddard (Captain), C. L. Walcott, E. Weekes, A. L. Valentine.

Glasgow

West of Scotland, Cricket Ground
Site of the first football international.

Partick

Right:

The West of Scotland Cricket Club was founded in 1862 in the suburban village of Partick to the north-west of central Glasgow by a group of local businessmen under the presidency of Colonel Buchanan, later Sir David Carrick Buchanan. In the early days, because of the facilities and support, the ground was used for many other events. From 1870 to 1872 Scotland played England in association football international matches at Hamilton Crescent and the 1876 Scottish Cup Final between Queen's Park and Third Lanark was staged at the ground. From 1870 to 1939 Hamilton Crescent was the home of the West of Scotland Rugby Football Club and four Scottish rugby internationals were staged on the ground rather than at Murrayfield in Edinburgh. Australian touring teams have been frequent visitors to the cricket ground, lastly in 1989 when the attendance was 3,500. This picture shows a view of the ground in 1914. *Murray Collection*

Above:

A view of the ground in 1988. *Author*

Torquay

Above:

The home of Torquay Cricket Club, the Recreation Ground is sited adjoining Torquay Rugby Club and only a cricket ball's throw away from the sandy beaches of Torbay and the Devon Riviera. Torquay has staged several cricket festivals in addition to hosting some of Devon CCC's matches in the Minor County Championship, Gillette Cup and National Westminster Bank Trophy. The ground has also been used by the Minor Counties Cricket Association for matches with touring teams, the last being against the New Zealanders in 1978. In August 1994 the Minor Counties Cricket Association will host a first-class match against the touring South Africans at Torquay. This view shows an aerial picture of the ground in 1959 during a Minor County Championship match. *Aerofilms*

Above right:
A view of the pavilion and scoreboard in 1993. One significant change since 1959 is that the wicket has been turned by 90 degrees. *Author*

OTHER PUBLICATIONS BY THE AUTHOR

TRENT BRIDGE

CRICKET PAVILIONS
by William A. Powell
A series of 20 cards

Compiled by the author, this high quality set of full colour cards contains each major county cricket pavilion plus Oxford, Cambridge and Arundel. Each card has potted historical information printed on the reverse side.

The Pavilion at the Racecourse Ground, Durham City. Co. Durham

DURHAM COUNTY CRICKET CLUB
Inaugural first-class season

A fine series of postcards in full colour depicting the seven grounds that were used by Durham C.C.C. during the 1992 season. Brief historical notes on the reverse of each card by William A. Powell. Supplied with presentation envelope printed with the County crest.

Available from County Print Services,
74 Walden Way, Hainault, Ilford, Essex IG6 3BJ

APPENDIX
BRITISH ISLES
FIRST CLASS CRICKET GROUNDS
(1801 TO 1993)

PLACE NAME	GROUND NAME	HOME TEAM	MATCHES FIRST	LAST	TOTAL FIRST-CLASS MATCHES	FIRST-CLASS COUNTY MATCHES
Aberdeen	Mannofield Park	Scotland	1930	1957	2	
Abergavenny	Pen-y-Pound	Glamorgan	1983	1993	9	9
Aldershot	Officers Club Services Ground	Hampshire	1905	1964	9	5
Alton	Municipal Recreation Ground	Hampshire	1904		1	1
Arundel	Arundel Castle	Sussex	1990	1993	4	4
Ashby-de-la-Zouch	Bath Grounds	Leicestershire	1912	1964	43	43
Aylesford	Preston Hall Ground	Kent	1846	1847	2	2
Ayr	Cambusdoon	Scotland	1958	1974	2	
Banstead	Recreation Ground	Surrey	1984		1	1
Barnsley	Clarence Ground	Yorkshire	1862		1	1
Barwell	Kirkby Road	Leicestershire	1946	1947	3	3
Basingstoke	May's Bounty	Hampshire	1906	1993	36	36
Bath	Lansdow CC Ground	Somerset	1844	1884	3	1
Bath	Recreation Ground	Somerset	1897	1993	242	242
Beckenham	Foxgrove Road	Kent	1886	1905	15	14
Beckenham	Lloyds Bank Sports Ground	Kent	1954		1	1
Belfast	Ormeau	Ireland	1926	1971	8	
Benenden	Hemsted Park	Kent	1843		1	1
Birmingham	Edgbaston	Warwickshire	1886	1993	1118	1073
Birmingham	Mitchell's & Butler's Ground	Warwickshire	1931	1961	13	13
Blackburn	Alexandra Meadows	Lancashire	1932	1935	4	4
Blackheath	Rectory Field	Kent	1887	1971	84	84
Blackpool	Stanley (Whitegate Park)	Lancashire	1905	1993	90	78
Blackwell	Miners Welfare Ground	Derbyshire	1909	1913	7	7
Bletchley	Manor Fields	Northamptonshire	1980	1987	3	3
Bournemouth	Dean Park	Hampshire	1897	1992	343	336
Bournville	Bournville Cricket Ground	Worcestershire	1910	1911	2	2
Bradford	Great Horton (Easby) Road	Yorkshire	1863	1874	8	8
Bradford	Horton Park Avenue	Yorkshire	1880	1993	311	303
Bramshill	Bramshill Park	Hampshire	1823	1826	4	3
Bray	Woodbrook CC Ground	Ireland	1907	1912	5	
Brentwood	Old County Ground	Essex	1922	1969	58	58
Brighton	Ireland Royal New Ground	Sussex	1814	1847	49	47
Brighton	Lillywhite's Ground	Sussex	1839	1842	2	1
Brighton	Royal Brunswick Ground	Sussex	1848	1871	64	59
Brighton	County Ground, Hove	Sussex	1872	1993	1042	1038
Bristol	Durdham Down, Clifton	Gloucestershire	1870		1	1
Bristol	Clifton College	Gloucestershire	1871	1932	96	96
Bristol	Ashley Down (County Ground)	Gloucestershire	1889	1993	674	671
Bristol	Greenbank (Packer's Ground)	Gloucestershire	1922	1928	20	20
Bristol	Broad Walk, Knowle	Somerset	1926	1928	3	3
Bristol	Imperial Athletic Ground	Somerset	1957	1966	9	9
Bromley	Philip's Field	Kent	1840		1	1
Bromley	White Hart Field	Kent	1841	1842	2	2
Burton-upon-Trent	Burton CC (Town Ground)	Derbyshire	1914	1937	13	13
Burton-upon-Trent	Ind Coope/Allied Breweries	Derbyshire	1938	1980	38	38
Burton-upon-Trent	Bass Worthington Ground	Derbyshire	1975	1976	2	2
Buxton	Park Road	Derbyshire	1923	1986	45	45

PLACE NAME	GROUND NAME	HOME TEAM	MATCHES		TOTAL FIRST-CLASS MATCHES	FIRST-CLASS COUNTY MATCHES
			FIRST	LAST		
Cambridge	Parker's Piece	Camb Univ	1817	1864	58	2
Cambridge	F.P. Fenner's Ground	Camb Univ	1848	1993	805	8
Canterbury	Beverley Ground	Kent	1841	1846	15	10
Canterbury	St Lawrence Ground	Kent	1847	1993	437	396
Cardiff	Arms Park	Glamorgan	1910	1966	245	243
Cardiff	Sophia Gardens	Glamorgan	1967	1993	151	151
Catford	Private Banks Sports Ground	Kent	1865	1921	38	38
Chatham	New Brompton	Kent	1862		1	1
Chatham	Nore Command Ground	Kent	1926	1929	5	3
Chelmsford	County Ground	Essex	1925	1993	202	*202 *1 match by Middlesex
Chelmsford	Hoffman's Ground	Essex	1959	1961	3	3
Cheltenham	College Ground	Gloucestershire	1872	1993	288	288
Cheltenham	East Gloucestershire CC	Gloucestershire	1888	1903	2	2
Cheltenham	Victoria Ground	Gloucestershire	1923	1986	20	20
Chesterfield	Saltergate (Recreation Ground)	Derbyshire	1874	1875	2	2
Chesterfield	Queen's Park	Derbyshire	1898	1993	379	379
Chester-le-Street	Ropery Lane	Durham	1992	1993	2	2
Chichester	Priory Park Ground	Sussex	1852	1950	19	16
Chislehurst	West Kent CC Ground	Kent	1822	1838	10	5
Chiswick	Chiswick Park	Middlesex	1886	1887	2	1
Cirencester	Cirencester CC (Park) Ground	Gloucestershire	1879		1	1
Clacton-on-Sea	Vista Road	Essex	1931	1966	60	60
Cleethorpes	Chichester Road	Nottinghamshire	1980	1990	4	3
Coalville	Fox and Goose Ground	Leicestershire	1913	1914	2	2
Coalville	Town Ground	Leicestershire	1950		1	1
Coalville	Snibston Colliery Ground	Leicestershire	1957	1982	8	8
Coatbridge	Langloan	Scotland	1980		1	
Colchester	Castle Park	Essex	1914	1993	92	92
Colchester	Garrison A Ground	Essex	1920	1972	33	33
Coleraine	Lodge Road	Ireland	1987		1	
Colwyn Bay	Rhos Road	Glamorgan	1927	1993	12	10
Cork	Mardyke	Ireland	1947	1973	3	
Coventry	Bulls Head Ground	Warwickshire	1903	1992	15	15
Coventry	Rover Ground, The Butts	Warwickshire	1925	1930	10	10
Coventry	Morris Motors Ground	Warwickshire	1931	1932	2	2
Coventry	Courtaulds Ground	Warwickshire	1946	1982	56	56
Cowbridge	Cowbridge Ground	Glamorgan	1931	1932	4	4
Cowes IOW	J. Samuel White's Ground	Hampshire	1956	1962	7	7
Cranbrook	School Field	Kent	1850	1851	2	2
Cranbrook	Swifts Park	Kent	1862	1863	2	2
Crystal Palace	Crystal Palace Park	Kent/London Cty	1864	1906	*48	38 *33 matches by London County
Darlington	Feethams	Durham	1992	1993	4	4
Dartford	Bowman's Lodge	Kent	1806	1809	2	1
Dartford	Hesketh Park	Kent	1956	1990	33	33
Derby	County Ground	Derbyshire	1871	1993	593	591
Dewsbury	Dewsbury & Savile Ground	Yorkshire	1867	1933	53	49
Dover	Crabble Athletic Ground	Kent	1907	1976	106	106
Downpatrick	Strangford Road	Ireland	1983		1	
Dublin	College Park	Ireland	1895	1961	28	
Dublin	Rathmines	Ireland	1912	1979	9	
Dublin	Castle Avenue, Clontarf	Ireland	1964	1989	9	
Dublin	Sydney Parade	Ireland	1965		1	
Dublin	Malahide	Ireland	1991		1	
Dudley	Tipton Road	Worcestershire	1911	1971	88	88
Dumfries	Nunholm	Scotland	1988		1	
Dundee	Forthill, Broughty Ferry	Scotland	1924	1992	5	
Durham	University Ground	Durham	1992	1993	6	6
Eastbourne	Ashford Road	Sussex	1867	1873	2	2
Eastbourne	The Saffrons, Meads Road	Sussex	1896	1993	218	150
Ebbw Vale	Eugene Cross Park	Glamorgan	1946	1990	25	25
Edinburgh	Raeburn Place	Scotland	1905	1966	23	

CE NAME	GROUND NAME	HOME TEAM	MATCHES FIRST	LAST	TOTAL FIRST-CLASS MATCHES	FIRST-CLASS COUNTY MATCHES
burgh	Myreside	Scotland	1982	1990	2	
ton	Woodvale Road	Ireland	1979		1	
ham	Lower Avon Street	Worcestershire	1951		1	1
rsham	Mount Field	Kent	1876		1	1
estone	Cheriton Road	Kent	1925	1991	118	84
ne	Agricultural Showgrounds	Somerset	1932	1961	18	18
shiels	Mossilee	Scotland	1911		1	
shead Fell	Eastwood Gardens	Durham	1992	1993	3	3
ngham	Garrison Stadium	Kent	1937	1968	30	29
gow	Hamilton Crescent	Scotland	1911	1976	19	
gow	Shawholm	Scotland	1965	1979	3	
gow	Titwood	Scotland	1963	1986	3	
tonbury	Morlands Athletic Ground	Somerset	1952	1973	18	18
sop	North Road Ground	Derbyshire	1899	1910	14	14
cester	Spa Ground	Gloucestershire	1882	1923	56	56
cester	Tuffley Park	Gloucestershire	1923	1992	156	156
cester	King's School	Gloucestershire	1993		1	1
alming	The Burys	Surrey	1822	1830	8	3
alming	Broadwater Park	Surrey	1854	1854	1	1
vesend	The Bat and Ball Ground	Kent	1849	1971	145	143
nock	Glenpark	Scotland	1926	1972	6	
dford	Woodbridge Road	Surrey	1938	1993	72	71
sowen	Seth Somers Park	Worcestershire	1964	1969	2	2
fax	Thrum Hall, Hanson Lane	Yorkshire	1888	1897	4	4
bledon	Stoke Down	Hampshire	1806	1806	1	1
ow	Hammerskjold Road	Essex	1970	1970	2	2
rogate	St George's Road	Yorkshire	1882	1993	95	88
lepool	Park Drive	Durham	1992	1993	3	3
ings	Central Recreation Ground	Sussex	1865	1989	229	140
khurst	Hawkhurst Moor	Kent	1825	1826	2	2
nor	Town Ground	Derbyshire	1987		1	1
eford	Racecourse Ground	Worcestershire	1919	1983	6	5
ckley	Ashby Road	Leicestershire	1911	1937	19	19
ckley	Coventry Road	Leicestershire	1951	1964	17	17
ckley	Leicester Road	Leicestershire	1981	1991	11	11
eck	Recreation Road	Yorkshire	1868	1889	8	3
nsey	Tivoli Road	Middlesex	1959		1	1
sforth	Hall Park Ground	Yorkshire	1885		1	1
sham	Warham Court	Sussex	1853	1855	3	3
sham	Cricket Field Road	Sussex	1908	1993	83	83
dersfield	St John's Ground, Fartown	Yorkshire	1873	1955	75	51
	Hull Town CC Argyle Street	Yorkshire	1875	1879	4	1
	The Circle, Anlaby Road	Yorkshire	1899	1974	89	88
slet	Woodhouse Hill Ground	Yorkshire	1869	1872	2	1
d	Valentine's Park	Essex	1923	1993	106	106
ton	Rutland Recreation Ground	Derbyshire	1925	1993	92	92
gton	Cattle Market Ground	Middlesex	1864	1868	19	16
nington	The Foster's Oval	Surrey	1846	1993	1895	*1628 *1 match by Middlesex
ering	Town Ground	Northamptonshire	1923	1971	64	64
derminster	Chester Road North	Worcestershire	1921	1993	54	54
gston-n-Thames	Leyland Motors Ground	Surrey	1946	1953	16	2
caster	Lune Road Ground	Lancashire	1914		1	1
nington Spa	Arlington Avenue	Warwickshire	1905	1910	4	4
ds	Bass Headingley	Yorkshire	1890	1993	363	306
ester	Aylestone Road	Leicestershire	1901	1962	399	399
ester	Grace Road	Leicestershire	1894	1993	617	615
es	Dripping Pan	Sussex	1854	1860	2	2
on	County Ground	Essex	1886	1977	412	407

PLACE NAME	GROUND NAME	HOME TEAM	MATCHES		TOTAL FIRST-CLASS MATCHES	FIRST-CLASS COUNTY MATCHES
			FIRST	LAST		
Liverpool	Wavertree Road Ground	Lancashire	1859	1872	4	1
Liverpool	Aigburth	Lancashire	1881	1993	171	157
Llandarcy	BP Oil Refinery Ground	Glamorgan	1971		1	1
Llandudno	The Oval	Wales	1925	1928	3	
Llanelli	Stradey Park	Glamorgan	1933	1965	23	23
Londonderry	Beechgrove	Ireland	1963		1	
Long Eaton	Recreation Ground	Derbyshire	1887		1	1
Lord's	Old Ground, Dorset Square	MCC	1801	1810	47	
Lord's	St John's Wood Road	MCC/Middlesex	1814	1993	2579	*1180 *2 matches by Surrey
Lord's	Nursery Ground	MCC	1903		1	1
Loughborough	Park Road	Leicestershire	1913	1952	15	15
Loughborough	College Ground	Leicestershire	1928	1929	2	2
Loughborough	Brush Ground, Forest Road	Leicestershire	1953	1965	16	16
Luton	Wardown Park	Northamptonshire	1986	1993	8	8
Lydney	Recreational Trust Ground	Gloucestershire	1963	1969	8	8
Lytham	Church Road	Lancashire	1985	1993	8	8
Maidstone	Mote Park	Kent	1859	1993	207	207
Manchester	Botanical Gardens	Lancashire	1848	1854	5	2
Manchester	Old Trafford	Lancashire	1860	1993	1244	1160
Margam	Steel Company of Wales	Glamorgan	1953	1963	5	5
Margate	Clifton Villa Estate	Kent	1864		1	1
Melton Mowbray	Egerton Park	Leicestershire	1946	1948	3	3
Middlesbrough	Swatter's Carr	Yorkshire	1864	1867	2	2
Middlesbrough	Linthorpe Road	Yorkshire	1882		1	1
Middlesbrough	Acklam Park	Yorkshire	1956	1993	42	42
Midhurst	Cricket Ground	Sussex	1830		1	1
Moreton-in-Marsh	Batsford Road	Gloucestershire	1884	1914	6	6
Mousley Hurst	Cricket Ground	Surrey	1806		1	1
Neath	The Gnoll	Glamorgan	1934	1993	42	42
Nelson	Seed Hill	Lancashire	1925	1938	9	9
Newark-on-Trent	Kelham Road	Nottinghamshire	1856		1	1
Newark-on-Trent	Elm Road	Nottinghamshire	1966	1978	11	11
Newport IOW	Victoria Recreation Ground	Hampshire	1938	1939	2	2
Newport	Rodney Parade	Glamorgan	1935	1965	27	27
Northampton	County Ground, Wantage Road	Northamptonshire	1905	1993	842	842
Nottingham	The Forest	Nottinghamshire	1827	1837	6	2
Nottingham	Trent Bridge	Nottinghamshire	1840	1993	1358	1300
Nuneaton	Nuneaton CC Weddington Road	Warwickshire	1912	1914	3	3
Nuneaton	Griff & Coton Ground	Warwickshire	1930	1989	26	26
Oakham	Oakham School Ground	Leicestershire	1935	1938	4	4
Oxford	Magdalen College	Oxford Univ	1829	1912	70	
Oxford	Bullingdon Green	Oxford Univ	1843	1843	2	
Oxford	Christ Church College Ground	Oxford Univ	1878	1961	37	
Oxford	The University Parks	Oxford Univ	1881	1993	693	
Oxford	New College Ground	Oxford Univ	1906	1907	2	
Pagham	Nyetimber Lane	Sussex	1976	1979	2	2
Paisley	Whitehaugh	Scotland	1952	1960	6	
Perth	North Inch	Scotland	1909	1970	6	
Peterborough	Town Ground	Northamptonshire	1906	1966	46	46
Peterborough	Baker Perkins Sports Ground	Northamptonshire	1967	1969	3	3
Petworth	Petworth Park	Sussex	1824	1826	3	3
Petworth	Petworth Park New Ground	Sussex	1844	1849	4	1
Pontypridd	Ynysangharad Park	Glamorgan	1926	1990	40	40
Portsmouth	US Recreation Ground	Hampshire	1882	1993	323	303
Preston	West Cliff	Lancashire	1936	1952	5	5
Prince's	Prince's Ground	Middlesex	1872	1878	37	18
Reigate	Priory Ground, Bell Street	Surrey	1909	1936	5	1
Rochdale	Sparth Bottoms Road	Lancashire	1876		1	1
Romford	Gidea Park	Essex	1950	1968	34	34
Rushden	Town Ground	Northamptonshire	1924	1963	22	22

PLACE NAME	GROUND NAME	HOME TEAM	MATCHES FIRST	LAST	TOTAL FIRST-CLASS MATCHES	FIRST-CLASS COUNTY MATCHES
St Leonards-on-Sea	Old Racecourse	Sussex	1857		1	1
Sandgate	Sandgate Hill Ground	Kent	1862	1863	2	2
Scarborough	North Marine Road Ground	Yorkshire	1874	1993	371	205
Selkirk	Philiphaugh	Scotland	1963	1971	2	
Sevenoaks	Sevenoaks Vine CC	Kent	1827	1829	4	4
Sheffield	Hyde Park Ground	Yorkshire	1830	1853	20	12
Sheffield	Bramall Lane Ground	Yorkshire	1855	1973	405	396
Sheffield	Abbeydale Park, Dore	Yorkshire/Derbys	1946	1993	40	*46 *2 matches by Derbyshire
Shireoaks	Steetley Company Ground	Nottinghamshire	1961		1	1
Southampton	Antelope (Day's) Ground	Hampshire	1842	1884	33	33
Southampton	Itchen (Day's) Ground	Hampshire	1848	1950	3	3
Southampton	County Ground	Hampshire	1885	1993	517	517
Southborough	B.M. Close's Ground	Kent	1867		1	1
Southend-on-Sea	Southchurch Park	Essex	1906	1993	121	121
Southgate	John Walker's Ground	Middlesex	1859		1	1
Southport	Trafalgar Road Ground	Lancashire	1959	1992	36	36
Stockton-on-Tees	Grangefield Road	Durham	1992	1993	4	4
Stourbridge	Amblecote	Worcestershire	1905	1981	61	61
Stourport-on-Severn	Chain Wire Club Ground	Worcestershire	1980		1	1
Stratford-upon-Avon	Swans Nest Club	Warwickshire	1951		1	1
Stratton-on-the-Fosse	Downside School	Somerset	1934		1	1
Street	Millfield School	Somerset	1961		1	1
Stroud	Erinoid Ground	Gloucestershire	1956	1963	14	14
Swansea	St Helens	Glamorgan	1912	1993	380	378
Taunton	County Ground	Somerset	1882	1993	667	666
Tonbridge	Angel Ground	Kent	1869	1939	106	106
Torquay	Recreation Ground		1954	1976	11	
Town Malling	Old County Ground	Kent	1836	1890	14	14
Tunbridge Wells	Higher Common Ground	Kent	1844	1884	36	28
Tunbridge Wells	Nevill Ground	Kent	1901	1993	162	162
Uxbridge	Uxbridge CC Park Road	Middlesex	1980	1993	27	27
Wakefield	College Green Ground	Yorkshire	1878		1	1
Welbeck	Welbeck Abbey Cricket Ground	Nottinghamshire	1901	1904	2	2
Wellingborough	Town Ground	Northamptonshire	1929		1	1
Wellingborough	Wellingborough School	Northamptonshire	1946	1991	43	43
Wells	Rowden Road	Somerset	1935	1951	11	11
West Brompton	Lillie Bridge	Middlesex	1871		2	1
Westcliff-on-Sea	Chalkwell Park	Essex	1934	1976	69	69
Weston-Super-Mare	Clarence Park	Somerset	1914	1993	188	188
Whalley	Station Road Ground	Lancashire	1867		1	1
Winchester	Green Jackets Ground	Hampshire	1875		1	1
Winchester	Winchester College	Hampshire	1875		1	1
Wirksworth	Derby Road Ground	Derbyshire	1874		1	1
Wisbech	Queens Road	Cambridgeshire	1867		1	1
Worcester	County Ground, New Road	Worcestershire	1899	1993	938	937
Worksop	Town Ground	Nottinghamshire	1921	1993	43	43
Worthing	Manor Sports Ground	Sussex	1935	1964	43	43
Wrecclesham	Holt Pound Cricket Ground	Surrey	1808	1809	2	2
Wrotham	Napps	Kent	1815		1	1
Yeovil	West Hendford	Somerset	1935	1939	5	5
Yeovil	Johnson Park	Somerset	1951	1967	12	12
York	Wigginton Road	Yorkshire	1890		1	1

The above 280 grounds have been used for first-class matches in British Isles from 1801 to 1993.
The number of matches played by one of the first-class counties is shown where appropriate - these totals refer to matches versus all first-class opponents.
Cambridgeshire matches (4) versus Cambridge University at Fenner's and Middlesex (20) versus the MCC at Lord's are not included in the county totals.
Grounds used for first-class cricket other than by all first-class counties, Wales, Scotland and Ireland are not include in this listing.
The total of all first-class grounds used has been 343 as at 1993.
* Note: this includes county matches v all opponents (ie touring teams, universities are included).

ABOUT THE AUTHOR

William Powell was born in Lahore, Pakistan in 1964 and has had a life-long interest in cricket.

He has been an avid collector of cricket books and memorabilia since the age of 13 and has acted as the Official Scorer to the Pakistan and Sri Lankan Test teams in England.

He is a member of the MCC, Middlesex CCC and Surrey CCC, together with several other counties, The Cricket Society, The Cricket Writers' Club and The Association of Cricket Statisticians & Historians.

Other books by the author include *The Wisden Guide To Cricket Grounds* (First Edition 1989, Second Edition 1992), Association of Cricket Statisticians *Cricket Grounds of Middlesex* (1990) and *The South Africans in England 1894-1965* (1994).